Talking To Spirits

The Key to Managing Your Future

Book 3 of the Spiritual Rescue Technology Series

By David St Lawrence

DEDICATION

This book is dedicated to all of my readers
who wish to learn the truth
about their immortality.

Every time we talk to a spirit
we are talking to another immortal being.

We have a lot of catching up to do.

Table of Contents

Spirits You Cannot Handle Alone.........158

xi

PREFACE

There are hundreds of books written by people who claim to have had encounters with spirits, and after reading quite a few of them I found it was easier to get accurate information about spiritual behavior by talking directly to spirits myself.

Everything in this book comes from my conversations with spiritual beings during thousands of counseling sessions. You will see material here which you will not see anywhere else.

I teach you how to communicate with spirits in this book and once you learn how to do this, you will be able to confirm for yourself what I have written here.

The first thing you need to understand is that you, yourself, are an immortal spirit who is currently running a body.

What is a Spirit? The best definition I can give you at this time is that you are a living thought.

All spirits are living thoughts. The spiritual universe is a universe of thoughts.

To restate what I said earlier, you are a living thought running a physical body. You are immortal. Your body is not.

You are surrounded by immortal spiritual beings who are much like you, but for one reason or another do not have bodies at this time.

This book is about the many ways these spirits influence and control you.

1

There are many different names for spirits, but they are merely different *names* for spiritual beings. *They are not different types of beings.*

Some of the names for these spiritual beings include: ghost, demon, haunt, specter, poltergeist, psyche, soul, entity, body thetan, wraith, shade, phantasm, and apparition. They are actually just beings with different experiences.

To keep things as simple as possible, in this book they are all called spirits or spiritual beings.

In these thousands of sessions with spirits I discovered what help they truly wanted and what information they were willing to share.

These sessions were friendly conversations rather than formal interviews and yet I was able to discover that spirits are an inexhaustible source of information about anything that beings have ever done anywhere.

Once you start talking to spirits, you will find that spirits will continuously present you with more data than you expect.

After reading this book, you will be able to verify for yourself anything you read or hear about spirits or immortality.

*There are many different names for spirits,
but they are merely different names for spiritual beings.
They are not different types of beings.*

*Some of the names for these spiritual beings include:
ghost, demon, haunt, specter,
poltergeist, psyche, soul, entity,
body thetan, wraith, shade, phantasm, and apparition.*

In this book they are all called spirits or spiritual beings.

*All spirits are living thoughts.
The spiritual universe is a universe of thoughts.*

*You are a living thought running a physical body.
You are immortal. Your body is not.*

*If you read and understand this book,
you will be able to communicate
with any of the spirits mentioned above.*

INTRODUCTION

This is a handbook on how to make friends with spirits and get them to assist you in making life easier. This book is a natural outgrowth of the Spiritual Rescue Technology I developed for use in my world wide spiritual counseling practice.

If you wish to dig deeper and examine the source material for this book, read the Appendix - Spiritual Rescue Technology.

The Appendix also contains a number of success stories that illustrate the life changing properties of this technology.

I reorganized and repackaged some of the original research in a form that makes it most useful to the person who wishes to teach themselves this technology and use it by themselves to change their lives.

I have included examples from actual sessions so you can see that talking to spirits can improve your awareness and cheer you up so you can enjoy life.

It is my hope that this will serve as a guide to developing an effective relationship with your spiritual companions and will allow you to accomplish goals that are otherwise unachievable. It may also provide a foundation for you to do your own research into the outer realms of the spiritual universe.

There are an infinite number of spirits we can encounter but it is useful to arrange them in a limited number of categories based on our ability to interact with them and benefit from that interaction.

The book is presented in four parts, which are based on your ability to deal with spirits:

1. Spirits you can talk to safely

2. Spirits who can help you and may already be trying to help you

3. Spirits you cannot handle without help from a trained counselor

4. Advanced concepts (Akashic Records) for observing the past, present, and future

YOUR CHOICES IN DEALING WITH SPIRITS

You are surrounded by spirits in the first three categories described above, so there is no chance of avoiding them, but you can manage the effects that any of these three groups can create on your life by your choice of lifestyle and your willingness to train yourself to talk to spirits. Here are a few lifestyles that people have chosen to deal with spirits.

1. Ignoring those Voices in Your head

If you choose to ignore the voices in your head and focus on your work or on raising your family using will power and personal rituals to calm your restless spirits, you will enjoy moments of clarity and peace even though you will continue to be troubled when your spiritual companions are triggered into action by events you cannot control.

This is the state many people try to maintain if they can. Unfortunately, the voices continue to affect you even when you refuse to listen to them.

2. Chanting and Praying to a Higher Power

You will find no lack of gurus and spiritual leaders to lead you in various rituals involving chanting and prayers.

There will also be leaders who will show you practices to open your third eye and to alter your consciousness with and without drugs.

Aside from the danger of putting you under the control of a hostile spirit, these activities generally provide a sense of relief by taking your attention off your problems rather than providing a way to solve them.

We have found that taking your attention off your problems merely prolongs the condition you are avoiding and eventually worsens them. We have found no cases where this solved problems, it only delayed the handling of the problems.

No matter how hard you try to focus on the important things in life, people will continue to irritate you by their behavior and you will not be happy with what keeps occurring.

3. Choosing a Life of Serenity

If you can choose a life of serenity and contemplation complete with Zen gardens or daily prayers as in a monastery, you are not likely to be doing anything which will disturb your spiritual companions in any of these three categories. Life can remain calm as long as you continue your ritual undisturbed.

Any attempt to expand your activities to embrace the issues of modern professional life will trigger spirits in all three categories. A life of serenity is not possible as a working professional in the world of business. You should consider the next option.

4. Train Yourself to Talk To Spirits

On the other hand, if you read this book and understand it, you will be able to deal with all three varieties of spirits when you encounter them. Life will become much less stressful and you will find yourself accomplishing more with less effort and confusion than ever before.

By taking responsibility for the spirits who surround you and putting order into your life, you will find enjoyment and satisfaction that you will never experience otherwise.

Spirits are an integral part of every person's life.

Learning to work with them and harness their energy makes life an adventure instead of a burden.

HOW TO USE THIS BOOK

You might wish to read this book from end to end as a first step. This will give you a useful overview of the tools available to you for managing your future.

Once you have an idea of the scope of the book, you will find the Table of Contents to be a useful tool for locating the subjects you wish to examine in more detail.

For those of you who wish to pick up an instant overview of the most important points that are made in this book, there are *quotations* that summarize most of the important points made in the regular text. Once you have read and understood the *quotations*, you will have a framework for learning how to successfully talk to spirits.

The Alphabetical Index will help you locate all uses of unusual spiritual terms. If you are curious about Reptilians or past life incidents, you will be able to go instantly to where they are discussed.

Once you have read through the book, I suggest that you might want to intensively study the first group of spirits you will encounter: Spirits You Can Talk To Safely

A GENTLE WARNING FOR THOSE WHO ARE INTERESTED IN SPIRITUAL PRACTICES

You may have wondered why the title of the first section is "Spirits You Can Talk To Safely."

The reason for that wording of the title is that there are spirits you can contact who are happy to help you succeed, but if you are using drugs or other spiritual practices, you can attract spirits who can cause you to go insane before you sicken and die.

The spiritual world ranges from a friendly shallows full of caring spirits to an incredibly deep abyss of beings who can consider you a suitable subject for an extended experiment in mind control.

Exploring the spirit world is much like exploring the depths of the ocean. If you snorkel, you stay in shallow waters and you get to see coral and lots of beautiful fish and other marine life.

If you put on scuba gear, you can quickly go to depths where you will die at the slightest mistake. As a beginning diver, I went down the side of a reef to a depth of 100 feet and almost drowned because I did not know what I was doing.

You can easily find enough spiritual beings to work with merely by meditating. If you wish to explore the spirit world by taking drugs or participating in occult rituals, you can attract beings who do not have your best interests in mind. Please do not do this.

Spirits You Can Talk To Safely

In this part of the book, you will learn how to talk to spirits safely, help them, and make friends with them so they will contribute to your life. If you follow my instructions, you should not encounter spirits who can harm you.

WHERE TO BEGIN?

We are surrounded by immortal spiritual beings in every state of awareness imaginable. They have lived many lives and have all sorts of experiences that can be triggered by what you do in your daily life.

When you have read this book and completed the exercises, you will be able to verify for yourself that talking to spirits is not only possible, but will allow you to accomplish goals that you formerly thought impossible.

The spirits who surround you can influence you in many ways, such as your choice of friends, clothes, music, foods, and lifestyles. If your life is not going the way you want it to go, you can be assured that you have spirits who are messing with your choices and your behavior.

Some spirits who accompany you are fully awake and aware and are constantly sending you thoughts and emotions depending on what you are experiencing in life.

Occasionally, a spirit will create an actual voice that you can hear. Receiving one of these voice messages can be quite startling.

If you are exposed to people your spirits do not like, these spirits accompanying you will make you feel uncomfortable and put thoughts into your mind that those people are dangerous. This can cause an instant dislike for someone you have just met.

If you meet a person these spirits approve of, they can create a romantic feeling of such intensity that you will instantly fall in love with the person and find yourself doing things that you may regret later. Just like instant dislike, there is almost no way you can deal with this feeling rationally.

After reading this book, you will discover that you are being influenced by thoughts and feelings that are not your own. This book will give you the tools to take back control of your life.

When you finally realize how many of your actions and decisions have been influenced by the spirits surrounding you, you will regain a state of free will that few living people enjoy.

We are surrounded by spiritual beings,
and you are constantly receiving
their emotions and intentions.

Your attitudes, desires, and actions
are controlled by these other spirits
and until you learn to talk to these spirits,
your life will not be under your control.

Spirits are talking to you constantly.
This book will show you how to understand
what they are saying and how to get them
to help you achieve your dreams.

WHAT DOES IT MEAN, SPIRITS YOU CAN TALK TO SAFELY?

There are countless spirits who are clamoring for your attention and most of these are either helpful or need a little assistance from you to become much happier which will result in your becoming happier too. When your active spiritual companions are happy, you will be happy too.

The spiritual realm is vast and deep and you can consider it to be like an ocean with shallows you can frolic in and an abyss in which scary monsters can hide.

When you confine your spiritual conversations to the beings who are trying to get your attention during your normal life activities, you will generally not run into problems, as these beings want to participate in your life.

If you are participating in occult ceremonies such as Hermetic Qabalah, Enochian magic, Thelema, Voodoo, Ceremonial Majick, and Witchcraft, you stand a good chance of attracting beings who are able to control you. These beings will have a history of demanding sacrifices and satisfying cravings with the objective of carrying out purposes from earlier existences.

Even ceremonies for Opening Your Third Eye can cause lasting problems because of the risk of falling into delusion through allowing other spirits to control you and your perceptions.

Casting yourself into the spiritual realm with the intention of being guided by some spirit opens the door to being taken over by some spirit with less than helpful intent.

Doing this sort of activity under the influence of drugs is an open invitation to permanent loss of control.

You can look at these occult ceremonies as worse than opening yourself to communication with strangers on an unsafe internet site. Once you attract the attention of dangerous spiritual beings, your life may never be the same. You will get a reality on how unpleasant being haunted can be.

Before you begin talking to spirits in earnest, you will need to learn what **caring communication** is and how to use it.

If you encounter spirits who do not respond to caring communication, you need to immediately cease trying to communicate with them as their intent will be destructive.

If you follow the instructions in this book, your communications with spirits will be productive and you will find yourself with many new friends.

HOW TO KNOW WHEN A SPIRIT IS AFFECTING YOU

1. You experience thoughts and emotions that you cannot seem to keep under control.
Something happens and you get a strong emotional reaction to it that you were not expecting. You are reading a book, for example, and you find yourself breaking into tears.

Or, someone on Facebook makes a rude comment about something you value and you find yourself launching into a rage-filled response which can persist for days. Sometimes this response can permanently change your relationship with long term friends and associates.

Your spiritual companions can react strongly to things people say and do and you will experience their emotions as if these emotions were your own.

2. Are you feeling happy?
Let's do the simplest test of all: Are you happy with your life at this moment? If you are, then all of your spiritual companions that are awake are happy too! Congratulate yourselves on being in good shape and continue doing whatever you are doing that makes you happy. This is an extremely important point, because if you are not happy with your life, you are being affected by unhappy spirits.

3. Are you feeling unhappy or afraid or upset in any way?
Let us take a more usual situation: If you are feeling unhappy or afraid or upset in any way, even though nothing is currently threatening you, a spirit may be contributing to that feeling.

15

Try to locate where the feeling of upset or fear or unhappiness is located. It will probably be close to your body or inside it somewhere. The feeling may be accompanied by a pain or a mental image picture of some painful event.

If you can perceive a negative emotion or a pain or a mental image picture of something unpleasant, you have spotted a spiritual being who is putting out a telepathic message that he is not feeling well.

4. What about chronic pains or upsets?
Now you may say, "I am always feeling pains and having visions, so why are you saying that a spirit is responsible for what I am feeling? I get headaches all the time!"

If you are under stress because of your work or family life, your spiritual companions also experience that stress. As a result, they may be reliving abuse and punishment from their past lives and you get the feelings and images of pain they have experienced.

Upset spiritual beings can create almost every feeling and pain known to man when they recall events that have happened to them in the past. When this happens to you often enough, you think these are your pains because you can feel them.

When a being feels pain, all beings who are close to him can experience the pain telepathically. You probably did not expect that telepathy could hurt but it does.

5. How can we change what spirits are doing to us?
When you learn how to talk to spirits, you are able to make the pain or upset go away for the spirit and for yourself. It is a simple conversational procedure and we will be covering it in the next section and several other places in this book.

16

When a spirit is feeling some pain or emotion,
You will experience that pain or emotion
as if it were your own.

This is called misownership and is why you can
experience negative emotions and strange pains
even when there is nothing in your environment
that seems to be threatening you.

WHY SHOULD YOU BE TALKING TO SPIRITS?

1. They are an incredible untapped resource for you.
Spiritual energy is what causes things to happen in the physical universe. It animates you and all other living creatures. Your spiritual energy is affected by the spirits who surround you. When you persuade spirits to help you and flow life energy to you, you accomplish what you set out to do with very little effort.

Spirits can provide emotional support when you know how to talk to them. They can also align their intentions with yours so that what you intend will overcome all counter-intention that exists.

Spirits will advise you if you let them, and they are frequently a source of warnings about activities you may not be paying attention to.

When you are surrounded by friendly, helpful spirits, your spiritual welfare increases and good things seem to happen as if by magic.

When you are surrounded by unhappy, sad, or hostile spirits, your spiritual energy is lessened and life becomes grim and you experience unexpected failures.

I have been researching spiritual communication for more than 40 years and have found that communicating with spirits in a caring way helps them heal from past experiences and restores their free will and hope for the future.

2. You can influence them favorably.

When you gain the ability to talk with spirits, you are able to influence your spiritual companions to work cooperatively with you to achieve your goals.

When you are trained to talk to spirits, you are able to extend your managerial skills to the spirit world and enlist the support of beings with talents that complement yours.

3. You can remove emotional barriers to your success.

You are able to remove emotional barriers to progress that would otherwise stop you or discourage you from achieving your goals.

You are surrounded by disembodied spirits every moment of the day and they influence you through their thoughts and emotions. You can try to ignore these distracting thoughts and emotions by throwing yourself into work, but they are still out there and the effort to ignore them will eat away at your concentration.

If you are unable to talk to these spirits, you have no way to improve their state of mind and they remain fixed in an unchanging emotional state which is usually based on their last experience of life in a body.

You may try to shut these thoughts and emotions out with mood-altering drugs and alcohol, but eventually these thoughts and emotions can overwhelm you, and the results are usually tragic.

When we read about a talented writer or entertainer committing suicide, we see the results of not being able to handle the pressure of destructive thoughts and emotions.

When you are trained to talk to spirits, you can wake them up in a caring way and get them to realize that there is an endless future to look forward to which can include hope for creating a better life for themselves with or without a body.

Spirits can choose to go through endless cycles of life in different bodies, but some seem to prefer life as a disembodied spirit, possibly because of the freedom to be anywhere at any time. The one drawback has been the lack of easy communication with spirits who are occupying bodies.

Now that we can teach people to communicate with spirits, this drawback may vanish and we may see more spirits choosing to remain in a spiritual state and maintaining a productive working relationship with those in bodies.

4. You can benefit from information and skills that spirits have accumulated.
Spirits are immortal and they remember much of what they have accomplished in previous lifetimes.

They have all sorts of skills and information that they can share with us if we ask them politely. If you are open to listening to suggestions from spirits, you can transform your life with very little effort.

If you look at really creative people who seem to have an infinite capacity for implementing new ideas, you will find that these people are in touch with the spirits in their environment.

Now that more of us are learning to communicate freely with disembodied spirits, we are seeing greater cooperative interaction between us and our spiritual companions.

I would expect that we will begin to see a whole new group of "gifted" people who rely on spirits for enhanced abilities.

We have always been aware of gifted children with abilities far beyond what they could have gained since birth. Now we are beginning to see young children with abilities that exceed any single person's abilities and I feel we are seeing the appearance of children who can recruit talented spirits to assist them to carry out tasks that would stagger a trained adult.

One example of this is the youthful composer, Alma Deutscher, who exhibits different personas as she performs and directs performances of her works.

I expect that my students will acquire the ability to recruit spirits to augment their abilities and will work out how to keep their exchange in by increasing the abilities of the spirits they attract.

5. You Can Have Access To The Legendary Akashic Records
If I did not make it clear in the previous section, I will repeat it again: *Spirits are immortal and they remember much of what they have accomplished in previous lifetimes.*

The Akashic records are a compendium of all events, thoughts, words, emotions, and intent ever to have occurred in the past, present, or future. They are believed to be encoded in a non-physical plane of existence known as the etheric plane. The *Akashic Records* are the energetic *records* of all souls about their past lives, the present lives, and possible future lives.

You can read about the Akashic Records in Part Four of this book, Advanced Concepts For Observing The Past, Present, And Future

If you are having difficulty grasping how this relates to you, here is a simple test for anyone who has communicated with spirits:

- Does a spirit have a brain?
- Where does he store his memories?
- When you see a spiritual image, does it seem any different than your images?

Memories are not stored in your brain. If that were the case, the spirits you talk to would need a brain and they do not.

Memories are a spiritual phenomena, not a physical universe phenomena. The seem to be associated with the spirit who first experienced them and they also seem to be able to be copied and transferred between spirits.

There is a lot that is unknown about memories and this can be a fruitful area of study for future spiritual researchers. We knew we can recover memories from long dead individuals, but until recently we had not studied where these memories are kept or how they are recorded. The *Akashic Records* are the *records* of all souls about their past lives, the present lives, and possible future lives. We discuss these records in detail in Part Four of this book.

If you are trained to perceive spiritual communication,
and you communicate in a caring way
with your spiritual companions,
there is almost no limit to the opportunities
you can take advantage of.

Your spiritual companions can share their knowledge
with you, they can do remote observations
of events that are of interest to you,
and they can influence others
by interacting with the spiritual companions
of these other people.

Since the information from any one spirit
will be limited to the observations
made by that particular spirit,
you can verify the correctness
of any data you receive
by cross referencing information
from spirits on every side of particular issues.

You will soon have the opportunity to verify
for yourself anything you have ever read
or heard about spirits or the afterlife.

Welcome to an incredible adventure!

WHAT QUESTIONS DO WE ASK SPIRITS ONCE WE LOCATE THEM?

Talking to Spirits is not an interrogation. You should attempt to make it a friendly conversation if you can.

Spirits are beings much like you except they may not have been running bodies for a very long time. Most of them will not have had anyone to talk to for a very long time and their social skills may be rusty. They will usually respond if you mind your manners and use caring communication.

When you become aware of a spirit, your first question might well be, "Is it all right if I talk to you?"

Alternatively, you might start by introducing yourself and then asking the question, "Hi! My name is David. Is it all right if I talk to you?"

Most of the time, you will get a surprised response like, "Uh, OK." and you can safely continue to gather information using steps like these as a basis for proceeding: (The entire process is described later)
1. Is there some way I can help you?
2. How long has it been since you had your own body?
3. Is there some incident you still have attention on?
4. Was there something you did or failed to do that triggered that incident?
5. How did you justify what you did or failed to do?

As long as you use caring communication, you will find that the spirit will have no trouble sharing information with you because he has had no one to talk to for many years and he is desperate to communicate with you and be acknowledged.

*If you can strike up a conversation with strangers in a coffee
shop, you have the social graces to talk with spirits.*

*If you learn to use caring communication,
you will be able to handle spirits
and help them no matter what shape they are in.*

WHAT IS CARING COMMUNICATION?

Caring Communication is the exchange of information between
living beings with the intent to help the other being achieve a
higher state of existence.

Caring Communication includes paying attention to the being(s)
you are talking to. In summary, it includes good manners when
talking to any spirits.

Most of the communication you receive on this planet is NOT
caring communication. How can you tell? *If the communication
does not make you feel better and appreciated, it is not caring
communication.*

Caring Communication will make you smile and will relieve
stress and increase your willingness to participate in life. At the
present time, Caring Communication appears to be an ability that
can be learned.

Caring Communication includes paying attention to the other
party, and having the intention to cause understanding in the
other party.

But most important of all, Caring Communication includes
taking responsibility for the other person being addressed.

*Caring Communication has the intention
to help the other being
achieve a higher state of existence.*

*Most important of all,
Caring Communication includes
taking responsibility
for the being who is being addressed.*

IS THERE A SECRET TO TALKING TO SPIRITS?

Yes there is and it has to do with your ability and willingness to treat your spiritual companions as "real people".

1. Spirits are beings just like us, but they do not have bodies.
I may have to repeat this several times for full understanding, but spirits are exactly like you and I, but for one reason or another they currently do not have bodies.

Spirit, ghost, haunt, specter, poltergeist, psyche, soul, entity, body thetan, wraith, shade, phantasm, or apparition, are merely different names for a spiritual being. *They are not different types of beings.*

You are a spiritual being who is currently running a body. You are surrounded by spiritual beings who do not have bodies at this time.

When you talk to spirits, you are talking to beings like yourself who have all of the capabilities and defects that you have. You communicate with them using telepathy and they have a wealth of information they can share with you.

2. Use good manners when you are talking to spirits.
There is no significant difference between talking to your departed grandmother or talking to President Lincoln. If either of these spirits happens to show up, you can strike up a conversation with them if you mind your manners and have a topic in which they are interested.

27

Some people fail spectacularly at talking to spirits because they are trying to order them around as if these spirits are some sort of inferior creature.

Talking to spirits is the polar opposite of exorcism. Exorcists are trained to view spirits as devils or evil creatures and they try to drive the spirits away. This is a big mistake, as you will see later.

Spirits can find themselves in a bad way because of their past experiences, but none are intrinsically evil, just not in their right minds. Later in this book we will discuss how you can talk to disturbed spiritual beings and bring them safely into present time where they can create new lives for themselves.

If you view spirits as beings just like yourself but without a body, you will be operating in the correct state of mind to carry on conversations with these beings and to help them and receive help in return.

3. Caring communication opens the way to helping spirits.
It does not really matter if the spirit you are talking to is a gang banger who died in a drug bust a few years ago or was a Roman soldier who has been parked on an English hillside for a few thousand years.

If you approach the being in a caring way with the intention of helping him orient himself to his current situation, you will find that you can converse on a number of subjects and the being will wake up and find himself interested in participating in the 21st Century in a new role that fits his needs.

If you start thinking of these disembodied spirits as people who are still parked in time as a result of some serious incident, you will be approaching them in the proper spirit.

They are immortal, just as you are, and they are capable of playing an infinite number of roles in contemporary society. All you have to do is wake them up with some caring communication and they will soon be ready to learn about surfing and mountain climbing and running businesses and raising families again.

4. Recognizing spirits when they appear is a vital skill.
You would do well to develop your skills at recognizing spirits when they are present and be willing to strike up conversations with them, because you will be picking up spirits every time you visit a hospital or a battlefield or any place where spirits congregate. Your ability to converse with them makes it less likely that they will hang around you and leave you feeling depressed for no apparent reason.

Spirits are always around you and once you gain the ability to perceive them and chat with them about matters that concern them, you become cause over them and are able to guide them to find places where they can work out their destinies without imposing their confusions on you.

5. Helpful spirits can be an amazing asset.
For those spirits who have a desire to help you, you will be able to guide them in working with you to achieve your goals. Many of the spirits I encounter are ready to participate in my life, even though they are not interested in picking up a body.

These spirits find that working with a person who is aware of them and can communicate with them satisfies their needs for action and at the same time lets them take advantage of the freedoms that go with being a free spirit. They can work with you as they see fit and they are still free to roam the universe in search of information and beauty.

When you accumulate a group of these spirits, you can be in touch with activities all over the world and have the potential to spread your influence through them as well.

Spirits are definitely real people who have lived many lives and they may have abilities that your other friends do not have. They can be an amazing asset when you know how to communicate with them and motivate them to help you.

I may have to repeat this several times
for complete understanding,
but spirits are very much like you and I,
but for one reason or another they
do not currently have bodies.

Spirit, ghost, haunt, specter, poltergeist,
psyche, soul, entity, body thetan, wraith,
shade, phantasm, or apparition,
are merely different names for a spiritual being.
They are not different types of beings.

You are an immortal spiritual being
who is currently running a body.
You are surrounded by immortal spiritual beings
who do not have bodies at this time.

Use caring communication when you talk to them
and you should have no problem making friends with them.

HOW DO I START TALKING TO SPIRITS?

You have been talking to spirits ever since you could form words. You just did not realize that you have had an audience, unless you were one of those prodigies who could talk with invisible friends at an early age.

1. Start by listening to what they have to say.
You have also been subjected to an unending barrage of thoughts and emotions and mental images from your spiritual companions all during this lifetime and many before.

You probably did not realize that many of the ideas and emotions you feel every day are presented to you by your spiritual companions. They are presented on a stimulus-response basis every time you attempt to create something or expose yourself to a new stimulus.

Your spiritual companions are responsible for the continuing rush of images, ideas, and emotions that flood your mind when you are not focused intently on some project. You can change your life by listening to what your spirits are saying to you.

2. Be ready to join the conversation.
You can start talking to spirits when you are ready to hear what they have to say.

Talking to spirits begins with listening to what is already going on, just like joining conversations with people running bodies.

Talking to spirits also involves being willing to communicate in a caring way with the spirits who surround you.

The other essential part of talking to spirits is having something to say that they are interested in.

3. Practice focusing your attention with a simple form of meditation.

Since your spiritual companions are already sending you thoughts on a 24/7 basis, let us start with a simple exercise to see how much of their communication you are already receiving.

I want you to begin with a very simple form of meditation. Sit down and close your eyes and notice how many thoughts are chasing each other through your consciousness. Do not intervene or repress these thoughts, just sit quietly and observe.

If you have the patience to sit for 30 minutes or so, you might find that these thoughts seem to go away or go quiet.

This is not the point of this exercise. The exercise is complete when you realize that the thoughts that are impinging on you are not yours.

4. Cover your eyes for a fast start to talking with spirits.

Just a quick note that may help some of you who have difficulty perceiving spiritual communication.

I find that covering my eyes with the palms of my hands, blocking out all light as though I was in a sensory deprivation chamber, allows me to perceive thoughts that I had not been able to sense before.

The point I wish to make is that covering my eyes left me nowhere to look except into my spiritual space and it revealed lots of activity that I could not perceive with my eyes open. I went in session within a few seconds once I covered my eyes.

5. Learn to connect with your spiritual companions through spirit writing.

Once you have some certainty that some of the thoughts you are experiencing are not yours, let's move on to a more demanding exercise which will require a pen and paper.

Sit in a comfortable position and write this question down at the top of the paper: "Is there anything you would like to share with me?"

Now ask this question of the space around your body and notice the thought that immediately follows your question. Write that thought down and thank the being who responded to the question.

The response will be immediate and may only be one word, but it is important to acknowledge the thought as you receive it.

When you ask the question, you must ask it in a caring way with full intention that you want a response. If you get no response to your question, it will be because you do not understand that you are addressing a spirit like yourself and you are just going through the motions with little expectation that anyone will answer.

If you get a response to your question about sharing anything with you, be sure you acknowledge the answer as you write it down.

If you grasp the importance of caring communication and have asked the question with the intention that you are going to communicate with a spirit and help them, you will get a flood of information and you may even fill several pages with what the spirits want to share.

This is a very old spiritual practice, and it is called "spirit writing". It is the recommended way of communicating with helpful spirits called spirit guides.

6. Examples of spirit writing sessions

One of the reason spirit writing works is that spirits have been trying to communicate with us for years and most of us are too busy to listen to thoughts that are not our own. When you write down the thoughts you perceive when you ask the question, it lets the spirits know that you are receiving them and they often get very excited.

I have had people end up writing several pages of spirit communications because the spirits were so excited to be able to get their ideas across. The messages can be serious or seemingly frivolous. One girl got her first message and it was, "Fix your hair!" Another girl got a message about taking better care of herself.

When I first did spirit writing, I got several pages of messages about what I was doing and I noticed after we were finished that every paragraph was in a different handwriting! I had started writing in block capitals and changed to cursive writing for the next paragraph, then the writing got very scrunched together and later shifted to a tiny cursive handwriting.

I had no attention on the penmanship when I was writing, but the spiritual "voices" seemed to require different handwriting to convey their emotions.

I am writing about fifteen hundred words a day for different purposes and the information comes through automatically now. I think about writing on a certain topic and I get several suggestions on preparing the text and how to write the story. Once I start typing, my hands never leave the keyboard and the words just flow from my spiritual companions to me.

Because there are several of them working together on each article, some do the creative work and others seem to enjoy the editing which they do in real time without interrupting the creative flow.

We rarely do any rewriting, although we sometimes discover a paragraph which needs to be brought to the front and used as the opening paragraph or introduction.

7. Making this spirit writing part of your daily life.
If you do meditation each time you wish to contact spirits and then use spirit writing to capture what they wish to share with you, you will find yourself with more new ideas to express than you have ever had before. If you use caring communication for all spiritual communication, you should find that your spirits will be willing to help you and share ideas with you.

As time goes on, you will learn to organize your spiritual companions into an effective team and you will find that creative work becomes effortless because you will have other beings sharing your work. Harnessing the efforts of others has always been a desired outcome and when you learn to talk to your spirits, your team will become more and more effective.

8. Acknowledge all spiritual communications.
I cannot emphasize how important it is to acknowledge messages and other thoughts you receive from spiritual beings. An acknowledgment is a vital part of communication because it lets the other person know they have been heard and are important.

You can verify how important acknowledgments are by thinking of a person who does not consider you important enough to acknowledge you. You will find that you are unwilling to have anything to do with this person and would not be unhappy if they would disappear forever.

An acknowledgment can take many forms as long as it lets the other person know their message has been received and understood. It does not necessarily indicate agreement, but it does complete the communication cycle.

Talking to spirits is a learned ability.
Almost anyone can do it if they follow these steps.

1. *Begin by calming yourself through simple meditation*
2. *Use Spirit Writing until you can use telepathy directly*
3. *Use Caring Communication for all spiritual conversations*
4. *Acknowledge all communications from spirits*

TALKING TO SPIRITS IN A SOLO SESSION

There are many ways to contact spirits and have a conversation with them as we have described earlier. You can perceive them as you go through your daily routines, or as you do spirit writing, but to really help a spiritual being who seems to be in trouble, you need to do the following sessions steps which have proven to be the most useful.

Sessions can be done with the aid of a spiritual counselor, but you should learn to talk with spirits on your own as you will be doing this for the rest of your life.

The session may seem informal and conversational, but restoring a spirit's ability to exercise their free will takes the right intention and careful attention to details. Here are some of the most important details to remember.

1. Make sure the being needs and wants your help.
Do not assume that every spirit you encounter wants your help. You will encounter some spirits who seem to be in a very bad way, but you will encounter resistance and get nowhere if you do not make sure that your help is wanted.

The safest way to proceed if you encounter an unhappy or upset being, is to ask, "Is it alright if I help you?" or "Is there some way I can help you?"

If there is any resistance, a little communication will generally help you sort things out so you can continue. If you do not get the being's agreement, do not proceed as you may create a barrier to further efforts to help.

Far too many people suffer from what I have been calling a "Missionary Syndrome" which manifests itself as an inability to recognize that their efforts to help are unwanted and counterproductive.

This kind of person feels that, based on their personal experience, certain courses of action are necessary and desirable and they give advice and seek to enforce behavior consistent with their past experiences instead of what the person really needs and wants.

When you get some experience with talking to spirits in session, you will hear countless stories of well meaning healers and missionaries who died horribly at the hands of the people they set out to save. Failing to find out what those people really wanted caused most of the trouble.

Your efforts to help a spiritual being may trigger a negative reaction if he has been damaged by well-meaning efforts to "help" that resulted in worsening his condition.

Your efforts to help a being may trigger incidents where he tried to help and was punished for it.

You can avoid all kinds of difficulty by asking a spirit if it is OK to help him and making sure that he understands your intentions.

2. Make sure you are using caring communication.
There are many questions you can ask a spirit that can worsen his state of mind. MAKE SURE YOU STICK TO CARING COMMUNICATION.

Caring Communication has the intention to help the other being achieve a higher state of existence. Most important of all, Caring Communication includes taking responsibility for the being who is being addressed. Caring Communication also includes paying attention to the being(s) you are talking to. Caring Communication includes using good manners when talking to any spirits.

Ask only the questions needed to wake the being up and to get him unstuck from the incident he is fixated on. Asking questions to satisfy your curiosity about his life and times can trigger unhappy incidents and can even awaken other beings who can bring the helping session to a halt.

Once you have started a conversation with a spiritual being, do not shift your attention to someone else as it is bad manners and the being may refuse to continue.

If the being cannot answer a question, make sure he has had time to answer before rephrasing the question. Do not interrupt a being if he is pondering a question.

3. Get the being to recognize that he is separate from you.
There are a number of ways to do this by asking simple questions.

Introduce yourself and ask questions like these:
    "What is your name?"
    "How long has it been since you had your own body?"
    "How long have you been with me?"

39

This can be very fast or it may take some conversation before the being knows he is a separate being.

Once the being has given you enough information to show he is aware of his current condition, you can go on to the process of freeing him from whatever past incident is still controlling his thoughts and behavior.

4. Find the incident which is still controlling him.
Unless a being is fully in present time, he is stuck in some past incident and is being controlled by the forces of that incident and the decisions he made while the incident was occurring. He will still have the images and the sounds of that incident fresh in his consciousness.

For example, if he died in a car crash he will be living in the last moment of impact with the sounds and sights and forces he was experiencing. Any time you are in a similar car or situation, that incident will be triggered and he will relive the incident and you will feel the emotions of the incident as though you were reliving the incident.

To locate an incident which is controlling you, you can locate the being who is producing the feeling of the incident and ask him, "Is there some incident you still have attention on?"

You will usually get an image of the incident and some information about what happened. You may get a long story about how this incident has affected his life. Do not interrupt him. Let him say all he wants to say and then acknowledge him so that he knows you have heard and understood his tale of woe.

5. Get what he did to trigger the incident.

Once he has finished describing the incident, ask the being what he did or failed to do that triggered the incident. He will probably have more than one answer and will usually be able to tell you if you give him enough time to recover the data.

You may have to rephrase the question several times before he realizes that he was responsible for triggering the incident that changed his life for the worse.

He may have failed to check for danger, or he may have said something that made a higher official angry enough to kill him.

6. Get his justification for doing what he did and keep asking questions until he begins to laugh.

You will find that he committed the action that changed his life because he felt he had no other recourse. It may not have made sense at the time so he has buried it from his memory. Once you have coaxed him to recover the justification for his action he will experience great relief. At that point the incident will no longer bother him.

You will find out that what he did was not a major activity at the time. He may just have joined the Army to get away from farm chores and he ended up in the SS under Hitler. Or, he may have become a Scientology cult member because he thought the female recruiter was pretty. He may have crashed a spaceship because he was fondling someone in the control room rather than watching the screens.

As soon as he has told you the last justification, he will experience great relief and will no longer be fixated on the incident that has been controlling him forever.

You will find that he can now move up to present time and will be ready to consider a new life.

7. Set the being free.
Once the being has moved up to present time, you can ask him if he wants to help you or if he would like to start a new life for himself.

If he wishes to stick around and participate in your life, that is definitely a good thing. You should give him a job to do so that you use his talents and keep him productively occupied.

Quite often the being wants to strike off on his own. In that case encourage him to depart and to take any friends with him. You will be able to feel his departure when it occurs.

Sometimes a being will wake up and not know what he wants to do. In that case, I suggest that you send him to a peaceful destination where he can think about what he wants to do and will have all the time he needs to make a decision.

Deserted beaches are best for this purpose, although some spirits prefer mountain tops or quiet lakes.

STEPS FOR TALKING TO SPIRITS IN SESSION

1. *Make sure the being needs and wants your help.*
2. *Make sure you are using caring communication.*
3. *Get the being to recognize that he is separate from you.*
4. *Find the incident which is still controlling him.*
5. *Get what he did to trigger the incident.*
6. *Get his justification for doing what he did.*
7. *Set the being free.*

LOCATING A TROUBLESOME SPIRIT

From my recent research, I have discovered that it is easier to sort out a troublesome area by looking for the *emotion* that is generated rather than trying to identify the spirit creating the trouble.

If you are not feeling your best, try locating where your negative emotion is located. You may be surprised how easy it is to do this. For example, let's say you are feeling sad. Just relax and try to spot the location that feeling is coming from. It will usually be a location near the body, perhaps even inside it.

As soon as you do this, your tone level will immediately change and you will shift into mild or strong interest as you begin to describe what you are perceiving.

Once you have located and identified the spirit you need to communicate with, you need to validate them as someone worthwhile who has something to say. I have found that being willing to assume their viewpoint and treating them as equals has produced the best results.

This is caring communication. Everything you say or ask must be directed to gently increasing the spirit's awareness of who they are and what has brought them to this point.

In summary then, look for downward shifts in your emotion as the indicator of a negative spiritual influence. Following these changes invariably leads to detection and handling of the troubled spirit.

SOLO SESSION EXAMPLES

1. Negative Emotion About Another Person

I was thinking about a person I had contacted a few weeks ago and I could still feel some animosity when I did this.

I thought, "Where is this animosity coming from? I have never done anything to this person! I have never met her before!"

When I looked for the feeling of animosity, I found an upset spirit behind my head. This was a being who had jumped from her to me during the conversation a few weeks ago.

The being was hostile to me, but I wasn't getting much communication, just some smoldering hostility. I could not figure out what I could have done to this being.

Finally, I covered my eyes with the palms of my hands, blocking out all light, as though I was in a sensory deprivation chamber and the thought came immediately, "I haven't done anything to her.....recently."

The entire scene started opening up and I had a marvelous solo session on how I had cursed myself a very long time ago by selling one of my siblings into slavery. She had died and vowed to haunt me forever but had not been able to find me.

She had been hunting me ever since and when I had met the person she was attached to, she took the opportunity to jump from that person to me so she could wreak vengeance upon me. Once we uncovered why I had done this deed and what she had done that caused me to do the dastardly deed, this blew all of the charge for both of us.

She is now off somewhere starting a new life. My relationship with the person she was attached to has changed completely and there is no negative emotion as we have no spiritual connection now.

This is an example of how easily you can pick up a spiritual being from someone else.

2. Negative Emotion - Sweet Oblivion
A Negative Emotion Session is an effective tool for spotting and handling emotions that negatively affect your life. I was running a search for something that felt like sweet death and I uncovered a being who was definitely good at producing a seductive urge to let everything go and sink into oblivion. I have been experiencing this feeling for years and it was being produced by this being.

This sweet oblivion feeling is very hard to resist and I used to experience it when I was unable to get up early in the morning. It is like a craving for more sleep, but it is actually a craving for oblivion.

Sweet oblivion is the ultimate release from pain and suffering. Trying to wake up on certain mornings would trigger this emotion and the being would take over my motor controls and I would slump back in bed and go unconscious in seconds.

It is the ultimate release from pain and suffering and this being created this state for himself so that no one could revive him. He was being tortured and devised an escape from the situation he was in.

He said there is no torture in life with me, but being pulled out of a sound sleep triggers this old response. He has not played the body game himself for 21,000 years.

After I had finished handling the incident and waking him up, he left for Ocracoke Island in North Carolina. Since then I feel completely free of the urge to enjoy oblivion.

3. Cravings for Anything
A craving is an intense desire for some particular thing.

There can be many non-spiritual explanations for cravings, including dietary deficiencies, but when the body is fairly healthy, there still can be intense desires prompted by spiritual beings who seek a certain sensation as a solution for some long ago problem.

The desired sensation can involve food, sex, alcohol, cigarettes, drugs, or even out-of-body experiences. A person can train himself to resist a particular sensation, but if he is exposed to the desired sensation when he is not in full control of himself, he will succumb to the craving and will compromise his integrity. A successful follower of Alcoholics Anonymous does not allow himself to be exposed to alcohol as he knows he is only one step from drinking again.

If one cares to look at where intense desire originates to satisfy a craving, one will usually spot spiritual beings and clusters who have that intention and are powerless to resist it. They are like a group of your peers egging you on to do it and do it right now! They will augment their intentions with pleasurable images and sensations until your resistance breaks down and you indulge yourself in the sensation you crave.

Not all cravings are for physical sensation; some people want to immerse themselves in books or videos to experience the rush of emotions that comes from living some other life than their own. They want to inflow emotions as others desire to inflow sensations.

If you look at your own episodes of craving something, you will probably find that there are specific situations that trigger these cravings. If you were handling these cravings with conventional therapy, you might find ways to avoid the triggering situations.

Using Talking to Spirits counseling, you can let your craving for something build to the point where you have difficulty resisting it and then notice where the craving is located. You will generally find an spirit or a cluster wants something very badly and wants you to satisfy that need.

It may take more willpower than you have available to keep focused on the counseling process instead of satisfying the craving, and, if this is the case, note well the spirit causing the craving and call in a partner to help handle this entity.

When you start communicating with the spirit or cluster, it is helpful if you can find what the spirit is doing and how long he has been associated with you. You might be surprised to find that you have had similar cravings for many lifetimes.

When you find the incident that the spirit or cluster is stuck in, do not be surprised if it seems to have little to do with your particular craving. The spirit's apparent craving is a solution for a problem that never got addressed. Do not concern yourself if the incident has little to do with your present time craving; just get the details of the incident and what the being or beings did that caused it to happen.

About the time you are helping the being to look at the justifications for what he did, things will begin to lift and the being or beings will let go of the incident and get interested in what you are doing or in what kind of future they now have.

Do not end the process until all beings involved have no further attention on the incident, on getting even with anyone else, or on anything in their past. When they are eager to move on and explore, it is time to send them for a locational process at a beach, a peaceful mountainside, or even a shopping mall.

If you have handled the right beings, you will experience a lessening of the craving you had previously. I use the word "lessening" because there is often more than one being involved in creating a craving for something. Beings and clusters tend to attract each other if they have similar past experiences, and these associations can go back a very long way.

Once you have handled a being or cluster and have experienced a lessening of a craving, consider that a win and end off for the day. Do not attempt to continue and handle all beings and clusters with similar intentions and cravings or you will get an overrun phenomenon where the beings consider that the processing has gone on too long. Once that happens, you have upset beings to deal with and you will not enjoy the results.

If you end off when you or your spiritual beings experience relief, you will find that these beings will stay happy for some time after session, and they will be eager to pick up any remaining charge or upset when the next session begins.

You may have to run many counseling sessions to completely handle cravings for some substances—especially drugs, alcohol, and food.

If you proceed carefully and end sessions when the spirits are winning, you will find that eventually the cravings will diminish to the point where they can be completely controlled without significant effort.

At some point, you may have some realizations of your own and the cravings will vanish entirely.

You can pick up spiritual beings anywhere.
They are attracted to people for various reasons
often because you and they have had similar lives.

They have lived many lives and had many identities.
Do not be surprised if they do not resemble
the people you are used to seeing.

They have been many places you have never heard of
and their careers may be strange to you.

If you treat these beings with respect
and caring communication,
you will be able to help them
and set them free.

PROFESSIONAL COUNSELING SESSION EXAMPLES

1. Negative Emotion - Panic About Losing Things.
This has to do with a being who was accompanying a friend and causing her to panic when she could not locate things.
I had the pleasure of meeting and helping Inoye (Sounds like In-oy-ee) who lost his body under mysterious circumstances a very long time ago. He was astral traveling and when he came back, his body was gone and he was never able to find it again.

As a result of that unfortunate incident, he would freak out whenever he was around when something important was lost.

He has been with a friend of mine for some time and she has always gone into a panic whenever she could not locate something important. Recently, she lost the registration sticker for her car and went frantically looking through her office for several days with no result. I took her in session and located the source of her panic and it was Inoye.

He was most recently an African native who could do astral travel and did so without incident until his last astral travel when he came back and his body was gone and there was no trace of his body or of the lions who had been guarding his body when he traveled. He has been stuck in this mystery for a very long time.

All he remembered was being summoned to Mars to check on something and he was sure he had only spent a few hours doing this.

A few questions revealed he had been hypnotized while he was on Mars and he had spent a very long time on Mars before returning.

To find out why he, an simple African native, had been brought to Mars and been given an hypnotic implant I asked how long he had been an African native. He replied, "about 13 lifetimes".

Questioning further, we discovered he had once been a spaceship commander who disapproved of some harmful action he was being told to perform. He stole a pod and headed to Earth because it was well known to be an uncivilized planet full of outlaws and rebels.

He hid and lived simply as an African native who had psychic abilities, including the ability to control lions. When he would go astral traveling, he would get a pride of lions to guard his body when he was away.

Unfortunately, his former civilization was able to find him and summon him to Mars and implant him and wipe his memories of anything that would make him useful. When he was implanted, he lost contact with his body and lost control of the lions, who probably ate his body.

I was able to help him recover his memories and as a result he was no longer frantic about his loss. Once he lost his franticness, his host no longer felt frantic either.

Inoye is happy to continue helping his host for now. My friend no longer worries about losing things and is ready to go on with her life.

If you find yourself going into a panic when things don't work out the way you want, look for a being who is generating that panicky feeling.

2. Interviewing a dead Lhasa Apso.

I have talked to a number of dead pets over the years, but this one was more aware than most. His mistress was still stressed over his death and I agreed to talk to the being and help straighten things out.

I talked directly to this Lhasa Apso, who still follows his mistress around wherever she goes. The Lhasa Apso was quite aware of his situation and made an unhappy comment about his dog bed which I did not fully understand until his mistress said she had another new dog using that bed.

His mistress is on mood-altering drugs and is not able to perceive spirit voices easily, but the Lhasa Apso was not disturbed at this. He seemed to be quite content with his current role.

He was accompanying his mistress and would occasionally give her his opinion on what she was doing. He was able to make her aware of the fact that he was still with her, but her drugs prevent her from picking up the finer details of spirit communication.

She promised to do solo sessions to get in communication with him and the other helpful beings I had introduced her to.

3. A Typical Day of Spiritual Counseling Sessions.

Every session I deliver is different, probably because every spirit is unique.

3.1 I was preparing to get up and was in that half awake period when spirits often speak to me when I perceived the image of an Inuit woman who appeared to be about 40 years old. She started chatting with me about some things that were going on in my family.

This was an unusual conversation as I normally do not get a strong visual image of the beings I am talking to. After a few moments, she disappeared.

3.2. During my first session of the day, I encountered a learned Greek scholar who was scared of dogs and told me a tale of wild dogs chasing a man and killing him in the city. According to him, this was a problem at the time as dogs were frequently observed attacking people in the cities.

After handling this troubling incident for him, he left to investigate a career at Harvard.

3.3. During my last session of the day, I was handling a spirit named Alethia who had killed herself as Atlantis sank beneath the waves. As we discussed the final moments of the disaster, she woke up and noticed my cat Milo sitting near me. She immediately took over his body and raced him excitedly around the studio.

After circling the studio at high speed, she made him prance and leap as though he was a kitten and continued making him throw a small rug around and chase a cricket.

Alethia was so excited at being able to control a body again that she stayed with Milo for several hours more. I took Milo out for our daily walk and she was very much in evidence because he held his body differently than usual and he climbed about six trees instead of his usual one.

She seems to have left him for more interesting places because Milo is back to his old slow moving self and does not have the special energy he had when she was aboard.

Possessions by spirits occurs more often than you might imagine. I usually notice it when a spirit takes possession of a person and causes them to behave in ways the person would consider to be out of control. Strong drink and politics seem to trigger possession, perhaps because the normal social restraints are blocked.

Possession will be discussed in more detail in the third section of this book, Spirits You Cannot Handle By Yourself.

When a spirit tells you a story
and presents you with images,
it is important that you accept what they say
and acknowledge it.

Otherwise, you are stopping the being
from sharing his experience
and getting relief from the incident he is stuck in.

If you just listen and acknowledge
what the spirit has to say,
you will learn about things
that will expand your knowledge of
what has been happening in this universe.

As you speak to more spirits,
you will learn that these stories are real
and have happened over and over.

SPIRITS CAN ASSUME ANY IDENTITY

From the session examples I have provided, you can begin to get the idea that spirits present themselves in many different ways. As far as I have been able to determine, all spirits are able to assume any identity they wish, from godlike beings to mushrooms.

The spirits I have encountered are immortal and can remember life on other planets and in other universes. This certainly expands on the idea that there is one afterlife where we all go and live happily ever after.

The model of life that appears in session after session is that the being picks up a body at birth and has a collection of spirits that follow him from life to life. In session after session I find beings who have been with their host for many lifetimes.

You may be a little uncertain if you have lived before, but a few sessions with your spiritual companions will give you a new perspective on how many lives you have lived and how many different careers you have had.

When you discover that you are immortal and you are surrounded by many immortal spirits with memories of daring and dangerous lives, it becomes evident that there are many painful memories that can be triggered when you live dangerously.

If you have ever wondered why some small children are so naturally cautious, it is because their last lifetime was only a few years ago and the painful memories still remain.

After talking to spirits for a while you will get a new appreciation for what a fresh start can mean to a being, especially if they shut off memories of their past lives.

SESSION EXAMPLE - MERINA THE DRYAD

I first encountered Merina when I was giving a session to my friend Kathy.

Merina has been a dryad or tree nymph for a very long time. She tells me she was rescued by my friend Kathy from her efforts to sustain a grove of dying Eucalyptus trees in arid Oceanside, California last year.

She says the legends about dryads are only partly true. They can adopt trees, but do not die when the tree dies or is cut down. It is like us and our meat bodies. They generally stick with their tree until it perishes and then they find a new home.

Merina loves Kathy and her love for living things, but she visited me here in Floyd during one of our sessions and was captivated by the lush greenery that stretches out for miles and miles in all directions.

She has also realized that she is a spirit just like me and Kathy and the rest of us, not a special type of being but a being with a particular identity, that of a dryad. She has been wearing the dryad identity for what seems like millions of years and that started when she came to this planet from a place that was increasingly industrial and mechanical.

She had some history of running machines, essentially computer systems, in a manner similar to what people are doing today and calling it Artificial Intelligence. Artificial Intelligence (AI) is actually a very old concept as it is essentially indoctrinating a spiritual being into being an information provider such as an oracle or making it run machinery for production.

She evidently resisted that role and was sent here where she has been working with plants and trees for a very long time. She says these natural systems are infinitely more complex and interesting than mechanical and electrical systems assembled by humans.

Since she has arrived in Floyd and gotten to know what is going on, she has promoted herself to be my advisor on plants and other living things. I notice a new ability today to perceive the still, small voices of plants now which I have never done before.

In the past, I could only perceive their distress when they needed water or other care. Now I am able to perceive their emotions through her. She perceives the plant's emotion and state of awareness and translates that into terms I can understand.

She offers to help me with our cats too. This is good because I need to understand them better. Otherwise, I waste a lot of time trying to help them in ways they do not appreciate!

Merina likes the idea of teaching spirits to communicate better and is planning to be a long-term member of my spiritual team.

She says, "Keep Earth Green. Please!"

THE REST OF THE STORY OF MERINA

Since I wrote about my session with Merina, she has moved on to be with local people who are more connected with the earth and sustainable agriculture than I am.

Her interests were more aligned with natural systems than with teaching spirits.

I have noticed that when spirits are brought into present time, they become more mobile and tend to move on to new locations as the mood strikes them.

Once they recover their ability to exercise free will, they find new opportunities to explore.

If you want a spirit to hang around and contribute to your activities, you need to consult with them and keep them occupied with activities they enjoy.

Spirits will go through many changes after you rescue them.

When you talk to spirits using caring communication
you restore their ability to exercise their free will.

Their ability to create and innovate increases markedly.

They can be a tremendous help to you if you motivate them
but if they are not interested in what you are doing
they will move on to more interesting pursuits.

Do not expect them to stick around
if you are doing boring things!

WOULD YOU LIKE TO LIVE GUILT FREE?

There are many people who avoid wrongdoing, but who cannot rid themselves of the fear that they have done something that has made them feel guilty. This feeling of guilt is so common that it is exploited by others, like teachers and other authority figures, who use this to control them.

Thanks to our research in talking to spirits, we have made a stunning breakthrough which can enable you to free yourself from the ever present guilt that makes you quail before an accusing stare or any suggestion that you have done something wrong. This is the feeling of guilt that many people experience even when they have not done anything wrong.

These deep seated feelings of guilt make you flinch when some one says, "You came in 30 minutes late!" or "You took the last doughnut!" or "You forgot to put the seat down!"

These feelings of guilt cause simple queries to trigger all sorts of unpleasant defensive reactions. If someone says, "Where were you?" or "Aren't you going to the reunion?" you find it hard to give a simple and honest answer.

These deep seated feelings of guilt will also cause you to lie when it is not necessary. Instead of telling the truth, you find yourself inventing all sorts of excuses and white lies. What is cvcn worse, these feelings of guilt cause you to anticipate being caught and your demeanor will project guilt when it is not necessary.

You will also find that people will not believe you because you are projecting guilt even when there is no actual reason you should feel that way.

Well, it's time to change your life and live guilt-free. With our recent spiritual research, I have been able to locate the source of this guilt and to provide lasting relief in just one or two sessions. If you have deep seated feelings of guilt that have been with you for years regardless of your actual behavior, you are afflicted with some spirits who are stuck in a mistake that has left them permanently feeling guilty.

Because you have been feeling their guilt, you have been influenced into acting guilty and have probably made mistakes and even fudged the truth to cover these mistakes up.

I have developed a way to locate these beings and free them from the trap of endless guilt that they have been carrying. You can start living guilt-free immediately and will shortly find yourself living fearlessly.

You will also find that your position in any group you are a part of will change for the better. You will find that you are becoming cause in your relationships rather than continuing to be the effect of others' opinions.

If you have deep seated feelings of guilt
that have been with you for years
regardless of your actual behavior,
you are afflicted with some spirits
who are stuck in a mistake that has left them
permanently feeling guilty.

Because you have been feeling their guilt,
you have been influenced into acting guilty
and have probably made mistakes and
even fudged the truth to cover up these mistakes.

When we handle the mistakes these spirits have made
we remove the guilt they have been sharing with us.

Our lives and theirs change for the better.

SESSION EXAMPLES - GUILT

1. Constantly Feeling Guilty About Everything

A friend of mine had her first session last week in which we located and handled a spiritual being who was so buried in guilt that my friend felt guilty all of her life and never knew why.

The being affected every part of my friend's life and made guilt a permanent part of her personality. It was so bad that she would lie without cause to cover up her feelings of guilt and avoid being blamed.

When you absolutely, positively KNOW you are guilty of something, life can become a living hell.

Every question, every questioning look, even an unfriendly glance, would trigger a feeling of guilty terror which made her feel uncertain and under attack. She always felt nervous because she did not know what was coming next and she constantly made mistakes and desperately wanted to cover them up.

When I located the frightened being and handled his mistake and the reason he made it, her personality began to change.

The guilty being left within minutes of being discovered and my friend immediately became calmer and more confident. She has maintained this new state ever since.

Today, she was returning a borrowed cup and bowl to a neighbor and both broke because of a mistake she made. For the first time in her life, she did not feel guilty because she had made a mistake. She felt a wonderful sense of relief.

No guilt, no blame, just an immediate solution. She is going to buy replacements. This is an ability that everyone can use.

2. Worried About What Others Think Of You?
You may have a spiritual companion whose desires are not aligned with contemporary society.

You might have a spiritual companion like Zack, whom I talked to recently. He had a long and colorful history of not fitting into regular societies because of habits he picked up in a very early society.

In the earliest society he remembered, long ago and very far away, the rules for social and sexual intercourse were mostly concerned with doing whatever felt good. These good times produced offspring with genetic difficulties and over many generations rules were developed that limited sexual relationships so that healthy children would be born.

Zack, however, was a being who found it hard to limit his sexual attention to partners approved by the groups he was a part of. He continued to have sex with his mothers, sisters, aunts, cousins, brothers, and fathers down through many generations of bodies.

Lifetime after lifetime he would engage in sex with members of his extended family and would eventually suffer the consequences. As he invariably came to into conflict with other members of every group he was a part of, he was increasingly worried about what people thought of him, but he could not change his behavior.

At some basic level he could not feel that he was doing anything wrong. His basic mode of operation was, if it feels good, do it!

I asked him what gender role he had preferred over these many lifetimes and he realized that he really had no preference. He just wanted to enjoy the start of the reproductive process.

I asked him how he felt about being a dryad or tree nymph of a garden or grove of trees in which he could be involved in the fertilization and blossoming of many plants at once. This role aligned with what he wants to do and he went off in search of the right garden to pervade and control.

Zack's former host now feels very little concern about what others think of her and in addition she no longer feels inappropriate sexual impulses like the ones she had to resist before.

With a being like Zack attached to you, you may have an unwanted state of sexual interest that has to be continually suppressed and a continuing worry about what others are thinking of you.

The bottom line is if you feel a sense of guilt that does not go away, it is worth investigating and handling any beings who are expressing that guilt. Worry about what others think about you is just a higher harmonic of guilt.

You should be able to live fearlessly with no attention on what others think of you. Handling your troubled spiritual companions will get you to that point faster than you realize.

SESSION EXAMPLE - DESPAIR

That feeling of despair you have been fighting may not be your own.

Have you ever tried to rebuild your life in a new area and been dogged by a sinking feeling of despair? You are not alone in this, but when you can talk to spirits, you have some unconventional tools to battle this despair.

In a recent session, a client found that his stomach ache and sinking feeling did not come from the usual causes of a bad meal or an upsetting phone call.

Instead, he found he was carrying the remnants of a catastrophic defeat on an English battlefield. He had been carrying this cluster of spirits for hundreds of years and the cluster contained dead soldiers from both the victorious side and the defeated side.

In dealing with battles, you might want to consider asking for participants from both sides of any battle you encounter. It would be a shame to free up one side and leave the others upset and unhandled where they could come back to create problems for you.

Whenever you encounter a cluster formed from a battle, you also might want to ask if there was a betrayal involved. Inevitably, you will find that one side or the other was sent into battle without full information of what they were facing and with assurances of support that would never materialize.

Wars are a particular form of insanity in which innocent lives are sacrificed to achieve a political end that violates every aspect of common sense and fairness. The historical accounts of this battle showed that the instigator of the campaign, of which this was the final battle, was effective in arousing support but poor in executing winning strategy.

He attended the battle, but fled in defeat after his army was crushed in about an hour. Like our late President Kennedy, at the Bay of Pigs, his planning was incomplete and the loyal people who believed in him were killed.

The defeated beings we handled were more than happy to seek out new lives after being stuck in this loss and betrayal for hundreds of years.

The dead victors had resented the orders they were given to kill all of the wounded after the battle was over.

Once again, the men who were doing the fighting and dying were mere pawns whose lives were being spent by higher ups to achieve hidden political ends.

They are all at the beach now, on one of the Hawaiian Islands.

When many beings have died at once
they tend to stick together
with their attention still stuck on the incident
and that moment of time.

We call that collection of beings a "cluster"
because they are still stuck in that moment of time
and react as if they were one individual.

When you contact these beings, their mental
voices will sound like a chorus
but you will be able to free them
and send them on their separate ways
if you use the regular process steps
and remember to use caring communication.

You can find more information about clusters
in Part Two - Beings Who Can Help You

VICTIMHOOD

Victimhood is the unhappy condition of considering that you are being oppressed by others or by situations in life. It can easily be restated as considering that others are responsible for your present condition.

Since this is a falsehood that is being held in place by you and your spirits, it can often be handled in very few sessions.

If you do not consider yourself as a victim, congratulations! You can read the rest of this article and see how it applies to those you wish to help.

If someone finds themselves saying or thinking any of the following ideas, they may have unknowingly slid into a state of victimhood:

1. You have been mean to me!
2. They have been mean to me!
3. My sister, friend, son, neighbor. etc. keeps unloading their problems on me and I am tired of it!
4. People in our group do not follow the rules and it makes me unhappy!
5. I expected more people to show up at our event.
6. People aren't buying art these days. (Substitute houses, insurance, your company's products. etc.)
7. Any statement at all that assigns responsibility for the state you or your family are in to someone else.

Now, if you recognize yourself or someone else holding the viewpoints expressed in these statements, you need to locate the spirits who are holding that viewpoint and get them unstuck from the incident that made them feel like a victim.

It may not immediately fix the situation, but it will free your attention and enable you to come up with solutions and implement them.

Friends do not let friends play the victim card.

*When anyone you know or you yourself
are stuck in an unpleasant mood
and can't seem to get out of it,
look for the spirits who are stuck in that mood
and talk to them until they feel better.*

*When you learn how to do this,
your life becomes better immediately.*

THE IMPORTANCE OF SHOWING GRATITUDE

This is actually an advanced concept which will get described in greater detail in the section of the book covering Beings Who Can Help You, but it is so vital that I am showing you how to use it here.

There are a number of spiritual practices which involve showing gratitude to higher powers or the universe at large. Some involve rituals and others just require you to express your gratitude to the universe or to God on a frequent basis.

Since I have learned to express gratitude, a number of "miraculous" events have occurred involving the arrival of new clients and increasing flows of income with no effort on my part. I clearly saw that expressing gratitude works and recommend that others learn to do this also.

When you express gratitude to the universe at large, you form attachments to those who are the recipients of your gratitude. You form bonds of affinity with them and you are both aware of each others presence on a continuing and pleasant basis.

In other words, you form a spiritual connection with others and they become part of your spiritual universe when you learn to express gratitude. This may seem esoteric, but it works without any need for a deeper understanding.

Constantly express your gratitude to the universe for what you are experiencing and life will be better and more rewarding.

A CHECKLIST OF NEGATIVE EMOTIONS TO SEE IF YOU ARE BEING AFFECTED BY SPIRITS

1. Your Habitual Negative Emotion May Not Be Visible to You

If you go around with a worried look on your face all day, you are probably not aware that you are doing it. Even if you are scowling, you may not be aware that you are doing so because that's just the way you feel all the time.

If someone asks you why you look that way, you will probably wonder why they asked.

Once again, let me remind you that your emotions are influenced or even controlled by the spiritual beings who surround you. If the influence or the taking over is temporary, you will probably notice that you are not being yourself at that moment.

If you are being constantly influenced by an unhappy spiritual being, you may be so used to it that it is not visible to you any more. Your friends and family may be so used to it that they no longer mention it either, but when questioned they will describe you as perpetually worried, unhappy, angry, or whatever mood you are stuck in.

We can handle this directly with spiritual processing now and that will open the door for you to get gains from counseling and solo sessions that were not available to you before.
Any being who is being continually triggered by your life style will tie up so much of your attention that you may not be able to get in session and benefit from any spiritual processing.

If your spiritual processing is not producing stable results, you really need to look at your habitual negative emotion and get that handled first. The following list was assembled from session results and is quite extensive, but is not complete.

2. Using the Negative Emotion Checklist
We are continually being influenced by the spirits surrounding us. The most significant aspect of this relationship is that we experience the emotions of these beings and think they are our own.

If you exhibit any of these emotions, locating and handling the spirits who are stuck in these states will effect an immediate and positive change in your behavior and this can be done in solo sessions. If you find yourself feeling angry about the inclusion of any of these emotions, you will benefit from running sessions on the beings with these emotions.

Pick any emotion you wish to handle and ask for the beings who are exhibiting this emotion. Run the Talking to Spirits processing on each being until it wakes up and leaves or joins the beings who are helping you. Since there can be more than one being exhibiting this emotion, it is suggested that you check for this emotion again in a later session to make sure that the emotional influence is gone.

3. Special Notice
If you can't spot a negative emotion on this checklist, but you do not feel cheerful and enthusiastic about life, you may be under the control of a spiritual being you cannot handle alone. This means that the spirit takes control of you and your life and during that time, your attention goes elsewhere and you have no recollection of what transpires when the being is controlling you.

When you are being controlled by a spirit with a habitual, fixed, or persistent negative emotion, the spirit's influence may not be visible to you, so I suggest that you ask someone you trust if you ever exhibit a negative emotion that you don't seem to be aware of. You may be quite surprised at what they tell you about your behavior because it may seem quite out of character.

If they give you an example of an emotion and you don't agree with what they have said, I suggest you get a session from a trained counselor and find out what is going on. You will be amazed at how much better you will feel afterwards.

Read the last section of this book, Spirits You Cannot Handle Alone, for more information about this phenomena.

NEGATIVE EMOTION CHECKLIST OF EMOTIONAL STATES

You will notice that this list does not correspond to other published lists of emotional states. These are the emotions we thought of or projected that led to discovery of upset spiritual beings. We assigned the names that produced reactions from spirits.

Once we realized that we could identify upset spirits by their emotional state, we explored emotions and attitudes that tended toward non-survival states and found that we could get responses from spirits who were stuck in those states.

Feel free to add others as you discover them.

Abandoned	Boring	Dangerous
Abased	Brazen	Dead
Afraid	Brutal	Unquiet Dead
Aghast	Brutish	Peaceful Dead
Alarmed	Can't Hide	Sweet Death
Angry	Captured	Sweet Oblivion
Animalistic	Caught	Defiant
Annoyed	Condescending	Degraded
Antagonistic	Confused	Delirious
Anxious	Confusing	Delusional
Apathetic	Controlling Bodies	Depraved
Apologetic	Covertly hostile	Deranged
Appalled	Cowardly	Despairing
Apprehensive	Cowed	Desperate
Approval from Bodies	Cranky	Despicable
Arrogant	Craven	Despised
Ashamed	Craving	Destructive
Baffled	Craving Drugs	Deviant
Banal	Craving Punishment	Devious
Bestial	Craving Sex	Disgusted
Beastly	Craving Death and Unconsciousness	Disgusting
Beautiful Sadness		
Being a ghost	Criminal	Disintegrated
Being an Object	Critical	Disinterested
Being Nothing	Crooked	Dismayed
Bitter	Crude	Disorganized
Bitterness	Cruel	Disoriented
Blame	Crushed	Disturbing
Bloodthirsty	Cursed	Doomed
Body Death	Damaged	Doubtful
Bored	Damned	Dying

76

Effeminate	Gross	Irascible
Embarrassed	Grumpy	Irresponsible
Empty	Guilty	Jealous
Enraged	Gullible	Judgmental
Envious	Hallucinating	Lascivious
Evil	Hateful	Lecherous
Exasperated	Haughty	Lewd
Exhausted	Hectic	Loathsome
Failed	Helpless	Longing
Failure	Hideous	Lustful
Total Failure	Hiding	Kinky
Fanatical	High (as in drugged)	Making amends
Fatuous	Homosexuality	Malignant
Fawning	Hopeless	Maniacal
Fear of Exposure	Horrified	Masculine
Fearful	Hostile	Mean
Feminine	Humiliated	Mechanical
Foolish	Hunger	Menacing
Furtive	Hungry	Mocking
Frenzied	Hysterical	Monotony
Frightened	Ignorant	Monstrous
Frightening	Imperious	Mournful
Frozen	Impulsive	Nasty
Frustrated	Indifferent	Nauseating
Furious	Indignant	Needing Bodies
Furtive	Ineffectual	Negative
Giddy	Inferior	Nervous
Gleeful	Inhuman	No Sympathy
Godlike	Insolent	Numb
Greedy	Insincere	Obscene
Griefy	Insipid	Obsessed

Outraged	Sacrifice	Spiritless
Owning Bodies	Sad	Spiritual Death
Pain	Self Abasement	Stingy
Panicky	Self Important	Stupefied
Paralyzed	Sexy	Stupid
Petrified	Shame	Submissive
Pitiful	Shameless	Suffering
Pitiless	Shattered	Suffocating
Pity	Shocked	Surrender
Poisonous	Shy	Surrendering
Pompous	Sick	Suspicious
Possessed	Sickened	Sympathy
Promiscuous	Sickly	Taunting
Propitiation	Simpering	Teasing
Protecting Bodies	Sinful	Tedious
Punishing	Sinister	Terrified
Puzzled	Skeptical	Thoughtless
Puzzling	Slave	Threatening
Rabid	Slavery	Timid
Regret	Supplicant	Tired
Repulsive	Sleazy	Trapped
Resentful	Sleepy	Treacherous
Resentment	Slimy	Unable
Unexpressed Resentment	Sly	Unaware
Revolted	Smarmy	Uncertain
Revolting	Smug	Unconscious
Ridiculed	Sneaky	Undeserving
Ridiculous	Snide	Unemotional
Robotic	Snobbish	Unexpressed Resentment
Ruthless	Snotty	Unhappy

78

Unreal

Unreality

Unsympathetic

Untrustworthy

Unwilling Slave

Unworthy

Upset

Useless

Vacant

Vacuous

Vapid

Vengeful

Victim

Vile

Vindictive

Vulgar

Wanton

Weary

Whimpering

Whining

Wicked

Willing Slave

Wimpy

Wooden

Worried

Worshiping Bodies

Worthless

Wretched

Zealous

HOW TO SEE IF YOU ARE BEING AFFECTED BY SPIRITS

1. Disclaimer

You do not have to believe any of this and should feel free to reject it or use it as you see fit. All of these observations are based on direct observations by a team of experienced spiritual counselors and clients.

If you have reached this point in the book and would like to see if you are still being affected by spirits, this checklist will give you some ideas for changing your life for the better.

Most of these observations are couched in terms of your personal experience, but you will see these manifestations in other people like your family members, friends, coworkers, and in elected officials, to name a few. The examples include things you see in yourself and in others.

Your behavior can be affected by your own painful experiences and decisions but your behavior CAN ALSO BE AFFECTED by the painful experiences and decisions of the spiritual beings who are associated and attached to you.

It has been observed that developing a working relationship with these spirits produces a happier existence for all concerned. Every being who has not been acknowledged is probably opposing your actions constantly.

Every being whose painful experiences are being triggered by what you do in life is causing you to experience the attitudes, emotions, sensations, and pains of these experiences as your own.

This effect is so pronounced that handling one spiritual being can change a person's life forever. I see this in session after session and I would like you to experience this for yourselves on a continuing basis.

This list describes indications that you may have some unhandled or unacknowledged spirits who are in need of help.

There are many more, but this should give you a good start. There are additional comments at the end which will help you get started handling your relationship with these spirits.

2. Warning – This is a "Hot" list and is not for casual reading.
If you get a significant reaction to this list, DO NOT keep reading to see if you can get more reactions. When you read this list and get a reaction of any kind, you have triggered a past experience of some being. Once you have woken a being up, you need to talk to him and see if you can help him recover his free will.

3. Follow this procedure to get best results.
This list should be run as follows:
1. Starting anywhere on the list, read down the list and take up the very first example that indicates to you.

2. Find the spirit that is reacting to the list, handle him and bring him to present time using the process described in TALKING TO SPIRITS IN A SOLO SESSION.

3. When you are finished, end session and enjoy your win.

When you are ready, start down the list again until you find another example that indicates. Spot the spirit, handle him and bring him to present time and take a break and enjoy your win.

You can do this over and over whenever you feel that there might be something to handle. Handling only the spirits that are awake and communicating makes talking to spirits a much simpler and gentler activity.

CHECKLIST OF BEHAVIORS

These are many signs of unhandled or unacknowledged spiritual beings. The indicators are grouped by function:

1. Inappropriate Emotional Reactions

A. You have occasional thoughts of committing suicide.

B. You feel overwhelmed and surrounded by confusion.

C. You are occasionally attacked by bouts of "beautiful sadness" when reading a book or watching a movie.

D. You have incredibly choreographed dreams with settings that reoccur frequently. You can wake up to go to the bathroom and then the dream will resume where you left off.

E. You feel paranoid with no observable enemies

F. You take tremendous satisfaction in exposing a clueless person who is doing something stupid.

G. You have recurring moods of feeling "undeserving" and "unworthy".

H. You have periods when you have extremely destructive thoughts about someone or something and you toy with various ways to kill them or utterly destroy them.

2. Distractions

A. You can't seem to finish cycles of action. You pick up the car keys and head for the garage and find yourself reading old magazines in the attic. You start to pay the bills and end up watching "NETFLIX" with no bills paid.

B. You are easily distracted. You start a sentence and lose track of where you were going.

C. You find yourself changing personality during a conversation.

D. You may feel you are watching your life from a different position.

E. You interrupt yourself with non sequitur statements or phrases during normal conversation.

F. You fidget intermittently, or your body jerks and can't be brought under control.

G. You have what is commonly called Attention Deficit Disorder, resulting from too many spirits trying to run your life.

H. You commonly use the wrong word, such as "think" instead of "thing". You continually misspell certain words.

I. You have a persistent "stammer". This means that you have a spirit who is constantly interrupting your speech. This makes it impossible to speak without a stammer.

J. Intending or attempting to do things but veering off and not accomplishing them.

3. Compulsions

A. You CONSTANTLY talk to yourself when working on something like cooking or puttering in the shop.

B. You talk to yourself about things that you already know.
Next time you find yourself saying,"OK, now the bills, OK, now to get a sandwich, OK, I should call that client, OK... Look around you and see who is listening or is giving you the script to say.

C. You pick at body parts compulsively. This can include biting fingernails, scratching yourself habitually, picking your nose, etc.

D. Random grimacing when there is nothing occurring in the environment.

E. You go into a hypnotic state when browsing Facebook or facing a TV screen and this will continue for hours.

F. You have songs that won't stop playing in your head. This can include ones that you make up.

G. You have a compulsion to eat certain foods.

H. You have a compulsion to be part of a group. Not just a desire to lead or be a member, but a compulsion so strong that it makes you subjugate the other parts of your life in order to be accepted in the group.

4. Aversions

A. You have an extreme reaction to perfumes or odors that others do not find repugnant.

B. You have extreme reactions to certain foods when there is no this lifetime exposure to the food.

C. You have a fear of certain animals when there is no prior contact with that kind of animal.

D. You have an extreme fear of spiders, snakes, etc. This is not just a dislike, but a fear that prevents you from dealing with them.

E. You have a fear of heights, caves, or being buried when there is no history of bad experiences of that type.

F. You have a fear of certain types and races of people when there is no prior contact with them.

5. Physical Sensations/Pains

A. You have recurring sensations and pains that turn on and off and continue this pattern for years even though you have had medical treatment for them.

B. You feel a pressure on your face that comes and goes when you have to confront something that is not pleasant.

C. While you were reading this list, an invisible force field exerted pressure on your face or head or you experience any other physical manifestation while reading this list.

D. You have persisting or recurring body problems that do not surrender to proper medical care and a healthy lifestyle

6. Inexplicable Events, Trends, Or Behavior

A. You feel like you are operating under a curse.

B. There are people in your daily life that seem to give you grief for no reason and you find yourself unable to deal with them although other people can do the same things and you will blast them away.

C. You keep committing harmful acts on yourself and on others.

D. You feel degraded and unclean.

E. You find yourself launching into the same story again and again. Sometimes with no recollection that you told it before.

F. You are able to rattle off facts in great detail with no evidence of ever using them.

G. You have dreams that come true, especially when the dream comes to pass in a place you have never been.

7. Messages/Warnings

A. You hear your voice reading to you when you read a book. If you try to read more rapidly as a test, the voice loses track and you get confused.

B. When you think some casual thought like "I should take the tomatoes out of the fridge", your mental voice says the thought along with you.

C. You occasionally hear your name spoken and you are all alone with no one around.

D When you read this list, you hear yourself or somebody else making comments.

E. The phenomenon of "mind chatter" is a classic symptom of spirits carrying on a conversation. You may not perceive this as separate voices but you are aware that something is being said.

F. Seeing things that are not there, or that are not visible to others. Trees transforming into people and addressing the person. People and animals appearing and then they are gone.

G. The feeling that an incident has happened before. (Deja Vu)

H. The occurrence of a noise, usually some sort of a snapping sound. This can occur at random or a fraction of a second after waking.

I. Frequently thinking "What shall I do?" "What should I do?"

8. Physical Universe Manifestations

A. Teleportation, things appearing or disappearing.

B. Spontaneous disruption of electronic communications, especially video conferencing like Skype or Zoom.

C. Things breaking unexpectedly at a moment of crisis.

D. Pictures falling off walls at the exact moment bad news occurs.

Summary

You should realize that a spiritual being is involved when you catch yourself doing one of these behaviors.

Spotting that a spirit is involved puts you in charge. You can let the spirit do things for you but you will be more at cause.

Acknowledging a spirit while he is at work can snap him out of the pattern he is stuck in. The spirit is going, "Oh my! I gotta stop him from doing that and changing everything!" and you go, "I GOT THAT" " THANK YOU" …..and there is this burst of surprise and your spirit may just wake up and get out of there in a hurry. If he doesn't leave, he will be much more likely to initiate a conversation with you.

If you see someone else doing any of the odd things in the current list, you may realize how much of other peoples lives are run by spirits.

If any of these points listed above indicated to you, see if you can get in communication with the spirits involved. A short session of talking to your spirits and your spirits will feel much better.

If you get a reaction, but you cannot contact the spirit involved, get help from a professional spiritual counselor who can deliver Talking To Spirit sessions. They will help you contact the spirit and free it from the incident it is stuck in.

IMPORTANT NOTE & DISCLAIMER

If, while reading this book,
instead of being excited at the prospect of talking to spirits,
you feel hopeless and unable to face
the idea of dealing with them.
You are already encountering spirits who can control you.

I suggest you turn to part three,
Spirits You Cannot Handle Alone.

If you are still hopeless after reading Part Three,
give me a call and get a free session
to handle the being who is causing that emotion.

CONGRATULATIONS!

You have now been exposed to enough information about your spiritual partners to enable you to speak with them and help them recover from past incidents so they can get on with their lives and create new futures for themselves.

With this information you can handle most of the ordinary spirits who accompany you through life. They are eager to make your acquaintance once you contact them and they respond to your efforts to assist them in a positive way. Once you are freed from their negative emotions, your life becomes easier and much happier.

Successfully talking to spirits produces two outcomes. Either the being regains his free will and decides to get on with his life and go elsewhere, or the being decides to stay with you and help you in whatever you are doing.

In your conversations with spirits, you may have observed that there is much more to be discovered in the spiritual universe. There are challenges which require assistance from a well trained spiritual counselor. There is also information which will enable you to become a well-trained spiritual counselor. There is a vast body of information available on training and organizing your spiritual companions into an effective team that can help you attain your life's goals in ways that will seem magical to those who cannot perceive and motivate spirits.

This important information is contained in part two - Spirits Who Are Helping You, and part three - Spirits You Cannot Handle Alone.

With the information you have read so far
you can handle many of the ordinary spirits
who accompany you through life.

The information in this next section
will enable you to understand and handle
spiritual situations you may not have
begun to think about yet,
like changing your personality
to become a winner instead of a loser.

Spirits Who Are Helping You

In this part of the book we will cover the anatomy of your personality and how you can change it to become the person you want to be. We will also be covering Life Force energy and how we can use this knowledge to heal bodies.

Finally, we will cover the recruitment and management of spiritual companions to build an effective team of beings who can accomplish whatever goals you wish to set.

WHO DO YOU THINK YOU ARE?

This section is going to test your sense of self and challenge some of your most cherished beliefs, but if you survive, you will gain abilities and emerge with an unshakable certainty of who you really are and what opportunities life can hold.

If you have been doing the exercises in the earlier part of this book and have talked to enough spirits to find some who want to stay with you and help you, it may have dawned on you that some of your spiritual companions seem to be awake and aware and seem to be helping you on a continuing basis.

Those of you who can successfully depend on your ability to create have an unlimited supply of ideas that seem to appear when needed.

Whether you work with art, music, words, or computer languages, you merely have to visualize what you want to create and complementary ideas arrive for inspection and evaluation. If you are paying attention to your sources of inspiration, you will spot that you have spiritual help.

Some of you may work with machines, either designing them or fixing them and merely have to look at a design or an existing system to have a solution or a fix appear in your mind. Once again, you will find that helpful spiritual companions are ready with suggestions for designing or fixing an existing design.

There are some people I know who can sense what is wrong with a broken machine merely by looking at it. They say they seem to have a spirit guiding them and they are right.

We are all surrounded by spirits, but some of these spirits are always awake and on duty. They are constantly in action and they function as permanent parts of our personality. Once we recognize who they are and what they contribute, and we are bright enough to acknowledge them for their help, we start taking advantage of their abilities.

It may take a bit of readjustment, but when you finally realize you are a composite personality consisting of a team of spirits working together, your abilities will expand like never before.

*Some of your spiritual companions
are awake and aware
and seem to be influencing you
on a continuing basis.*

*When you finally realize
you are a composite personality
consisting of a team of spirits working together,
your abilities will expand like never before.*

ANATOMY OF A PERSONALITY

A personality is defined as the set of emotional qualities, ways of behaving, etc., that makes a person different from other people.

Personality traits reflect a person's *characteristic* patterns of thoughts, feelings, and behaviors.

When you realize that a group of spiritual beings can act as if they are a single complex being, you can begin to understand that this is the true state of most people on this planet. Our personality is the composite of all of the awakened beings who accompany us through life. If we do not know how to control the group, mayhem can occur.

This behavior has been mapped by scientists for many years and various personality aspects and personality traits have been described in great detail. What has not been understood until very recently is that these traits are produced by separate spiritual beings and these traits change over time as spirits are added or leave or as the spirits involved are trained.

Our personality can be changed by training or by spiritual counseling directed at the beings who make up our composite personality. In the absence of counseling directed at shaping our personality, our behavior is a stimulus response pattern based on inputs from our environment and from our efforts to control our personality. If we make no attempt to control our personality, we see the result as mob rule by whatever spirits are able to take control.

95

Once you know how to talk to spirits and get them to help you, you have mastered the skills needed to change or optimize your personality to accomplish the goals you set for yourself.

A number of years ago, my friend Roger Boswarva made this interesting observation:

> In actuality, we as composite beingnesses with our teams
> are currently a rather rapidly changing "unit" . . . we are
> accumulating vast new knowledges and understandings
> along with new or recovered powers and abilities . . .
> hence the need for regular reviews to put all this change
> in place for proper upgrading and optimization.

Management of your spiritual partners, and therefore of your composite personality, is not a static situation. You need to review your approach to life and its challenges frequently and tune your personality to optimize your results from the efforts you put forth to achieve your goals.

Once you know how to talk to spirits
and get them to help you,
you will be able to learn the skills needed
to change or optimize your personality.

WHO SHOULD BE IN CHARGE?

Once you are proficient in talking to your spirits, and realize that you are a composite personality, life becomes a different game.

If you have studied the materials and have successfully run sessions, you become aware that your actions are influenced and occasionally controlled by the spiritual beings who accompany you through life.

So, who decides who is in charge of your life? In the best of all worlds, you should be in charge of your life with the helpful assistance of those spiritual companions who have skills that enhance your quality of life.

However, if you look carefully at your behavior this lifetime, you will undoubtedly note that there were times when you lost control of your actions and behaved in a manner that did not show off your best qualities.

I am sure you can spot times you suffered from stage fright, or shyness, or from uncontrollable anger when someone acted in a truly insulting manner to you. These reactions in most cases are generated by spirits who seek to protect you from harm.

When your environment becomes threatening, these beings automatically produce a response that was effective in handling some past threat. Essentially, they take control of your body and perform the actions that should handle the perceived danger.

These automatic responses can cause trouble for you when the present time threat is not life threatening. For example, some people get furious when someone makes them wrong by questioning their data, and they are unable to discuss the issue without getting abusive.

Once you become aware that some of your spiritual companions will react violently if challenged, you have an opportunity to handle this situation by talking to the spirits and addressing the causes of their upset.

You will learn over time that you need to monitor the actions of your spiritual companions while they are participating in contributing to your life. This will enable them to contribute while enabling you to maintain control.

You are already taking advantage of their contributions whenever you launch into a discussion that you have had before. Your word for word recounting of your adventures is a feature that certain spiritual companions excel at. If you find yourself effortlessly telling jokes or making humorous remarks, you are relying on one of your spiritual companions. All you have to do is think about the possibility of telling a story and it will automatically come forth.

To avoid boring your family and friends who have heard all of this before, you should shut down your storytelling spirit when he has delivered his lines enough times to a particular audience.

I feel that all habit patterns are powered by your spiritual companions. Once they figure out that you need to do something more than once, they do an excellent job of replicating the action over and over again without modification.

If you are wondering what I could possibly be thinking of, let's consider the following chores that your spiritual companions are doing for you every day: Putting on footwear, putting on pants, putting on a shirt, brushing your teeth, or driving to work on your daily commute.

You initiate these tasks in some way and then your attention goes on something else. I can almost guarantee that you do not know what sock or shoe you put on first. Similarly, brushing your teeth becomes automatic once you have placed the toothpaste on the toothbrush.

On commuting, you only get back in the loop and take control when there is a traffic problem or an intersection that your handy chauffeur-being can't handle. Most of the time you are driving, you are thinking about other things.

Some people seem to run their lives on automatic and when you talk to them you get canned responses for common requests and greetings.

If you stay in present time and monitor the activities of the beings who are willing to help you, you may get the best of all worlds. You do the management of ongoing activity and you solicit information from your spiritual companions on an as needed basis.

In this way, you present an image of focused awareness while having a deep knowledge about a wide variety of subjects on tap for immediate use.

I notice that when I am examining anything from a work of art to a Facebook article, I receive a running commentary from my spiritual companions about the subject I have attention on.

The commentary can contain observations about the tone level of the author, the inconsistencies in the story, and observations about the intentions of the publication, etc. The observations can include aesthetic judgments of art and even estimation of future effects on civilization.

The comments can be affirmative or critical, but they give me a wider perspective than if I was operating alone.

The point to be made here is that your spiritual companions can be a huge resource if you can learn to harness their willingness to help you.

In the best of all worlds,
you should be in charge of your life
with the helpful assistance of those spiritual companions
who have skills that enhance your quality of life.

You do need to stay in present time
in order to take advantage of their skills
and not be surprised by undesired contributions
which can diminish the results you wish to create.

What this means is
that you need to stay in the present moment
in order to benefit from the contributions
of your spiritual companions.

If you let them operate without supervision
they can make you say or do something
which you may immediately regret.

COMPOSITE PERSONALITY OBSERVATIONS

1. In many people, one being insists he is in charge and he maintains control by domination of all spiritual beings in his environment. He is not open to any new ideas as he operates off a rigid set of rules. This person will resist almost all spiritual activities that involve interaction with spiritual companions.

2. In other people, one being insists he is in control because he is unaware there are other beings affecting his ability to make decisions and causing him to exhibit different personality traits depending on external circumstances. The person in this situation does not believe in spirits.

3. Some individuals become aware of spiritual beings who are directly affecting them and strive to get rid of these beings as soon as they notice them. The more they do to get rid of these spirits, the more spirits become visible to them and the individual soon becomes frantic and eventually overwhelmed.

4. For some individuals, several beings struggle for control and the person exhibits different personality traits depending on external circumstances. This is generally a lifelong situation which began at birth.

5. Some spiritual individuals recognize they have helpful spirits, or spirit guides, who assist them in life and contribute significantly to the overall personality that is exhibited. These individuals may or may not realize that there are also disturbed spirits who affect their personality negatively.

6. A few individuals recognize they are a composite beingness with spirits of varying skills and abilities. These individuals may have an awareness that they are a team whose success depends on their ability to organize and to handle any spiritual beings who do not share the goals and purposes of the team.

As they gain awareness of their status as a team, this group becomes capable of changing the scope of their activity on a continuing basis. This can be considered a self-aware group of spirits and their success depends on their teamwork.

Conclusion: When you learn how to talk to spirits and set them free from past errors, you are free to craft the personality you need and want to accomplish your goals.

You can get a reading about your current personality by doing an online test
If you are interested in getting an external viewpoint of your current personality, take any one of the tests available for that purpose and see how you stack up today. The Myers Briggs (MBTI) test can be done quickly and produces results showing 16 Personality Types, of which some are listed here.
- The Inspector – ISTJ Personality.
- The Counselor – INFJ Personality.
- The Mastermind – INTJ Personality.
- The Giver – ENFJ Personality.
- The Provider – ESFJ Personality.
- The Idealist – INFP Personality.
- The Supervisor – ESTJ Personality.
- The Visionary – ENTP Personality.

If you feel that the results do not show the real you, look at the personality aspects that you resist and find the spirits who are projecting those values.

A few sessions dealing with these personality aspects and you will find that you can take this test again and your results will have SHIFTED!

I am including this to show that your personality is mutable, not that any test is valid for predicting your behavior.

You can get a reading
about your current personality
by doing an online test.

If you do not like what the results say,
try talking to your spirits until you get
the personality results you want.

You will find that your test results will shift
as you handle your spirits and their considerations.

Your spirits contribute to your personality.
Why not talk to them
and get the personality you need
to succeed in life?

WHERE CAN WE GO FROM HERE?

Once we realize we are not a single spiritual being running a body, we need to consider what approach to life makes the most sense to us.

1. Types of Spiritual Organizations

Some people just let life take them where it will and let whatever spirit wishes to take the helm do so. They do the best they can with whoever is running the show and only reorganize their spiritual activities when they run into difficulties. This group will find it will continue experiencing changes that it does not anticipate.

If a person knows he has spirits accompanying him and uses Talking to Spirits, he can handle and remove spirits who are not contributing to the success of the group. He has the potential to learn more about the group of helpful spirits and possibly organize them for more efficiency.

2. Self-Organizing Groups

A group of spirits that communicates freely with each other can become self-aware and will find that it can self organize and optimize results in more than one direction. In effect, the group can decide to change the group personality to achieve specific goals. This starts when the being running the body gets the rest of the spirits to communicate freely with each other and to see what they have in common.

A group of spirits that communicates freely with each other can decide to change its purpose, its membership, and its structure. This can be a fully informed decision resulting in significantly improved abilities to be, do, and have what the group wants, if the group continues to be fully self aware. The group can also elect to seek out and enlist spirits who can enhance the group's performance in specific areas.

A self aware group of spirits acting in concert can decide how to create an environment that is optimum for its purposes. It is not limited to reacting to external events - it can act to change them if it wishes. The rules for such a group have not been written yet, but will be developed as each of these groups emerges.

3. The Leadership Role Changes

Group leadership is a matter that has not been fully explored, but the question of who is in charge has been raised by clients and students for several years. Students have asked, "Who am I, if there are all these other beings in my space?"

I have answered, based on my earlier observations, that one being, usually the one who runs and owns the body, should be the ringmaster or the manager in charge of activities. In some cases, the person felt they were not up to the task and has abdicated leaving control to other beings. I now have more insight into the problem they were facing.

During a lifetime, your roles change depending on your environment and your body age. The personality aspects required for success in each of the phases of life can change also.

I have the feeling that different beings take over during certain phases of our lives in an effort to successfully cope with the stresses of each phase. When the personality of the being in charge suits the external circumstances, all goes well and the person has a reasonably successful life at that time.

If there is no available being with the right personality, another being attempts to handle the task and the results are less than satisfactory.

If the being currently in charge of the body was spectacularly successful as a student or young adult with ability to charm sexual partners and to carry off bold feats without showing fear, it may fail spectacularly as an elderly man with an old body. Instead of being able to project wisdom and compassion and earn the respect of his peers, he is still hitting on young women and trying to be the alpha male at every gathering.

In the same way, a woman who was the most popular girl in high school or college may find that she needs a different personality to succeed as a respected business executive.

If she has a suitable spiritual beingness on tap, she will make the transition easily. If she is still trying to be the most popular girl in the organization, she may not see the career success she wants.

4. Changing Leaders Successfully
These different personality changes are accomplished properly when there are beings standing by ready to take over when the moment is right. A new being takes command and life goes on in a new direction. The change in command has been generated by external conditions.

A self-aware group of beings acting in concert can respond to changing conditions, but they can also initiate changes to suit their own purposes when they desire to change the conditions of their existence.

This group can observe a relationship, or a career, or a state of existence, and decide to be whoever they need to be to accomplish the changes they desire. Choosing who you wish to be is really a matter of choosing who you wish to lead the group and getting everyone aligned for that purpose.

In other words, choose the being with the right personality for the situation and let him or her get on with it. As long as there is agreement within the group, all should be well. The rest of you can kick back and let the new guy take charge. If you have picked the right guy and support him, you are in for a good time.

5. Summary of a Successful Leadership Transition
In summary, if you want to change your personality to create a new existence, put a being in charge who has the experience and personality to carry off the new role. If you examine your past performance in a similar area, you will find the being who can manage the transition.

In a self-aware group, the lead can be passed to the being who can do the best job for a given situation. Different beings have different strengths. If your group is self aware, the strengths will be known by all concerned. Situations can change and the group should be prepared to assign command to the beings best suited to the situation at hand.

In a self-aware group of beings
acting as a composite personality,
the lead can be passed to the being
who can do the best job for a given situation.

Different beings have different strengths.
If your group is self aware,
the strengths will be known by all concerned.

Situations can change
and the group should be prepared to assign command
to the beings best suited to the situation at hand.

You are already doing this as you respond to life's challenges.
Why not plan ahead and create the personality
that will bring you success and happiness?

HISTORICAL OBSERVATIONS ON MULTIPLE BEINGNESSES

Psychologists have long recognized that there are different aspects to personality and one of the most recent models is the "Big Five aspects of Personality".

They have also recognized that some people can exhibit multiple personalities, as in MPD (Multiple Personality Disorder), and there is a great deal of historical evidence of these alternative personalities.

Sometimes patients will start with just 2 or 3 alter personalities and it will develop into nearly one hundred. It is common for those with MPD to have personalities of both sexes. In fact, multiple sex personalities are found in just about every patient that has MPD. There are even some patients that have alter personalities that are animals like dogs, cats, or some kind of farm animal. (https://www.psycom.net/mchugh.html)

After you have read and digested what psychologists have learned, you can verify for yourself that most personality aspects (multiple personalities) are in fact separate spiritual beings who can be communicated with and have individual histories separate from the host personality.

The simplest and most caring way to help a person with multiple personalities is to speak with any of the personalities who are willing to let you communicate with them. If you use caring communication, you will be surprised how well your communication is received.

INTRODUCING SPIRITS, LIFE FORCE, AND BODIES

1. Spirits Are Immortal And Predate Bodies

Once you get some experience talking to spirits, you will see that spirits predate bodies. In fact, you will eventually discover that some spirits predate the physical universe. You will also discover that you and your spirits did not originate on this planet. When you ask for the incident that a spirit has his attention on, you never know what will come forth. You should just take what the spirit gives you and carry on. You should never try to get the spirit to give you data that you are willing to believe in.

More can be learned about why spirits created and occupied bodies of various kinds in the first place, and since we are now spirits occupying bodies, I thought it might be useful to share what we have discovered so far.

Spirits are immortal, although we have some evidence that a spirit can adopt a state of non-beingness where he is non-sentient and almost nonexistent as a being.

We have not tried to rescue beings from this state, but I have some evidence that this state exists. I picked up a black tourmaline crystal and experienced a sudden discharge as all of the beings entombed in the crystal left. All that was left was a dead black piece of mineral.

You will discover that spirits can assume almost any state of mind and any state of awareness, from godlike to being dirt.

2. Life Force

Spirits emanate Life Force. They are the only source of life force. Life Force is the energy produced by spirits and animates all living things. Life force is known by more than 66 names: Qi, Chi, Prana, etc., but all names mean the energy that animates all living things.

Life force can be felt and observed. Every part of a living body emanates life force. When a body is damaged or dying, the life force is lessened or absent.

Spirits emanate life force in proportion to their spiritual health. As spirits dwindle from joyous exultation down to apathy and non-existence as beings, they emanate less and less life force.

Every cell of the body is a living thing and each cell contains spirits who animate the cell. The state of the cell can be determined by the life force that is animating it. Since spirits are the source of life force in the body, it means that caring for these spirits can improve the health of the body and all of its parts.

There are as many different ways to encourage the production of life force as there are ways to encourage spiritual welfare. Conversely, spiritual attacks on the spirits animating the body will damage the health of the body.

Expressions of love and tenderness convey a spiritual warmth that can practically reanimate a sick or damaged body.

Hate flows directed at a body or body part will actually cause damage over time. This can be observed with plants or animals as well. The intention to harm can be as damaging as physical harm.

I am sure you have seen people who can make plants flourish merely by directing love at the plant every day. Well, I have witnessed the opposite effect. I saw a teenaged girl cause a large plant to wither and almost die by the hate flows she was directing at the plant. When I spotted what she was doing and made her stop, the plant recovered. (She had no idea that she was capable of such psychic power.)

Bodies are spiritual creations and are powered by the spirits in every cell. If you want to have a healthy body, do your best to admire it and handle any source of spiritual upset you detect. You can talk to any of the spirits in your body and if you find some who are disturbed you can help them and restore health to that part of the body if the damage is not too great.

There are a great number of people who are natural healers and they do this by perceiving disturbances in the person's life force and flow healing energy to the injured or diseased body parts.

Once you start talking to spirits, you will find that you can see disturbances in a person's life force and with a little practice, you will find you can help the person recover, if they are willing to let you help them.

Do not attempt to heal someone if they do not want spiritual healing, as they will block your efforts and can even cause themselves to get sicker to prove you wrong.

Do not feel you have to limit your healing efforts to talking to the spirits involved. There are many ways to comfort ailing spirits: smudging with burning herbs, healing music, singing healing melodies, healing massage, laying on of hands and warm stones.

Once you gain the ability to see the fluctuations in a person's life force, you will know what increases life force and what does not. In some cases, medical care and drugs will help, but you will be able to monitor what is going on by observing what the person's life force is doing.

3. Spirits Seem to Need Games to Avoid Boredom

Spirits do not need bodies for many of the activities they can indulge in. They can travel instantaneously to any point in the physical universe in the past, present, or future. They have been able to create and destroy matter, energy, space, and time and although they are capable of infinite awareness and knowledge, they make mistakes and have lost a great deal of their original free will because of decisions they have made in the past.

From session data, it appears that one of the problems that can beset an all-knowing and all powerful being is boredom and in an effort to alleviate this boredom, the being begins to play games with other beings.

In order to play a game, beings adopt rules which require them to not know what the opposing beings know or are going to do. If all information and intentions are known, there is no possibility that an unknown result can occur. A game seems to require that the final result is unknown, therefore players in a game have to give up their ability to know what is going to happen.

To add complexity to a game, a being can define a playing field and create pieces or players to participate and to mark progress in the playing of the game. In this way, games can be devised which can take long periods of time and cover lots of physical universe territory.

Creating living pieces to use in playing a game seems to add a necessary degree of complexity that challenges a spirit. The ability to take perceptions and sensations from the body as it is used in the game keeps the interest high and is part of the reward from playing the game.

Spirits like games, and possession of a body evidently combines challenges and rewards of a grand nature. Depending on the game, a spirit may even be running multiple pieces or bodies and even playing their roles against each other.

Over time, the number of games can increase and sub-games can arise with goals and objectives that outreach any of the original goals. As the number of players is unlimited, the complexity of the games being played can increase without limit and the original point of the games can be lost in the shuffle.

Having pieces (bodies) with finite lifetimes adds to the complexity of the game of life. The game can be infinite, but your chosen pieces must be swapped out after a while and new strategies must be employed.

I see spirits who played grand roles in ancient history choosing to re-emerge in a role with great handicaps just to prove that they have what it takes to succeed under all conditions. A great leader with a stunning history of victories can choose to re-emerge as a crippled native boy or girl from a primitive culture to prove to himself that he can overcome all obstacles.

You can get the idea from these session observations that winning the great game is what is important and the body you use is just a tool for playing the game effectively.

Unfortunately, for many of the players I have met, the purpose of the great game has been lost over the eons and their attention is stuck on the impermanence and condition of the body they are running

Most of us are no longer players in a great game. We have become the pieces we were fielding. Over the eons, we have gone from gods to pawns and broken pieces on the chessboard of life.

Spirits emanate life force and animate bodies.
All bodies and body cells contain spirits.

When you learn to talk to spirits
you gain the tools to heal bodies.

You can tell when you are healing a body
because the flow of life force increases.

WHAT IS A BODY?

1. A Body Is Your Piece In The Game Of Life.
Without a body, you are limited to borrowing and driving someone else's body. Yes, there are beings who do this, but it is not considered fair in some circles.

Having a body is like owning a car. The condition of your body indicates a lot about your life style and what you consider to be important in life.

Since any being has the capability to take over a body that is left unattended, it is not recommended that you go astral traveling without making provision for protecting your prize possession. You would not leave your car unlocked and unwatched in most city streets because it would not be there when you returned.

Taking drug trips presents similar risks. Under the influence of some drugs, you lose control of your motor functions and your ability to reason. A hostile takeover by another being is a risk to be avoided.

Bodies allow you to experience sensations in concentrated form. All of the spirits running your body participate in the body's activity and you get the rush and excitement of eating food and experiencing pleasurable activities like sex and challenging physical activity like skiing and surfing.

116

Since your body is your key to participating in the game of life, you should know how to spot when something is wrong and how you can help it recover by talking to the spirits who animate your body and run the various subsystems of the body.

In this very next section, we will cover how you can talk to your body and to the spirits within it.

2. Who Is Running Your Body?
Your body is a complex organism consisting of billions of cells and at least 78 organs that are arranged to carry out the specific functions required for everyday living. Every part of the body is managed by spiritual beings who animate the body part.

The body is a system of systems. To get the right viewpoint about the body, you need to perceive the life forces coming from the various systems of the body, and from the parasites and bacteria colonies and the cancer cells in the body. All of these groups are alive and are in contention for control of the body. Each cell and groups of cells have spirits animating them and controlling them.

There may be a spirit who "manages" the body, but each time I contact a spirit acting in the capacity of the body's "soul", I find that being to be merely a caretaker with no real control over the body.

You do not have to be a trained shaman or medical doctor to make a change in the state of the body. When you touch a person's body with love, that communicates to the spirits in the body and it will produce a beneficial effect almost immediately.

Many people consider the brain to be the home of the soul. It is not. It seems to be more like a switchboard for the nervous system because when a person has a stroke, they lose control of their body but they are still able to think even when they cannot make the body communicate.

3. Perceiving Life Force In The Body
If you are able to perceive life force, you can look at a person's body and see where it is having trouble. With no formal medical training, you can use caring communication through physical or psychic means to reassure the body that help is at hand.

This is not medicine or the practice of medicine as we are not diagnosing or treating disease.

We are perceiving life force, which traditional medicine does not recognize as real, and we are communicating with our life force to the spirits inhabiting the body with the intent to bring them out of their unconscious state and into present time.

A body is a living system of great complexity which is being animated and controlled by spiritual beings residing in every cell. If we are able to communicate with spirits on a larger scale, we can train our attention on the areas of the body that are in trouble and seek to bring the spirits out of the incidents they are stuck in and gently into present time.

There are numerous ways to heal the body spiritually. You should feel free to use the method you feel confident in as long as you are making progress.

When body cells have been badly injured, the responsible spirits may be so unconscious that physical contact is needed instead of telepathic communication. Learning a variety of healing processes will give you the tools you need when a situation resists being handled in the usual ways.

In the next section, we will describe a few spiritual healing processes you can use for the majority of situations you will encounter in regular life.

You do not have to be a trained shaman
or medical doctor
to make a change in the state of the body.

When you touch a person's body with love,
that communicates to the spirits in the body
and it will produce a beneficial effect
almost immediately.

If you can learn to talk to spirits
your ability to heal increases
by orders of magnitude.

SPIRITUAL HEALING PROCESSES

Spiritual healing can take many forms and has been used effectively for thousands of years. Spiritual healing is the activity of making a person healthy without using medicines or other physical methods, sometimes as part of a religious ceremony.

Spiritual healing includes the following methods: Prayer, Visualization, Energy healing, Application of Psychic powers, and Direct conversation with spirits.

In this book, we will be discussing energy healing and direct conversations with spirits.

ENERGY HEALING

Energy healing focuses on the life force that flows through all of us; that force that dictates our mood, health, energy, and ability to connect with other beings. If you have read the earlier sections of this book, you have an understanding that life force pervades and animates all living things.

You may not have exercised this ability yet, but you can perceive life force with a little practice. First you need to put yourself into a meditative state by closing your eyes and relaxing until your thoughts settle down and you are free of head noise.

(If you have any difficulty meditating, refer to the section titled, How Do I Start Talking To Spirits, Practice Focusing Your Attention.)

Put your attention on the part of the body that is injured or is in trouble. You can do this with your eyes closed if that is less distracting. Focus your attention on the disturbed area and compare what you perceive there to the area away from the disturbed area.

It will not take long before you become aware that the troubled area seems to have a different color than the other area and the disturbed area will have a recognizable shape and size.

At this point, you should not try to mentally push or poke at the area, just observe it and see what emotions are coming out of the area.

Get the idea of sending a caring and healing flow to the injured area and observe what happens. If you have been able to do this without feeling any skeptical or hostile thoughts from your spiritual companions, you should sense a feeling of relief begin to appear in the injured area.

Continue the caring flows until the injured area returns to normal. It may take several sessions to create a complete recovery. If you have other people who are willing to join you in flowing caring flows to the injured area, you will find that the process will be accelerated.

Be aware that skeptical flows from the person you are trying to help or from onlookers will stop the energy healing. Skeptical flows are harmful as they intend things to stop and not succeed.

Spiritual healing is best done in a caring and safe environment. It takes a master healer to make progress in the presence of skeptics and hostile onlookers.

If you are trying to heal yourself and are not sure of your ability to heal, get help from a spiritual healer and you will find that your recovery is far more rapid. Also, the best way to learn spiritual healing is to watch it being done by someone else. Once you have seen successful spiritual healing, you will be more likely to be able to duplicate what has been done.

TALKING TO SPIRITS IN THE BODY

If you have read the earlier materials on life force, you will see that there are a lot of spirits animating a body and all of the creatures, bacteria, and parasites that occupy the body. You might well ask, where do we begin?

The answer is the same whenever we seek to talk to a spirit. We talk to the spirits who recognize our communication and who seek to communicate with us. This is actually simpler than it seems.

There are always spirits who are more aware than others and when you look into any area of your body, these spirits will be the first to send you a message or a mental image or an emotion.

Experienced physical therapists who pay attention to spiritual signals will often notice a problem area in a patient even before the patient mentions what is going on.

Once you start paying attention to your body and the spirits who inhabit it and animate it, you will realize that your body spirits are sending signals to you all of the time.

You do not have to have a knowledge of anatomy and organ structure to receive messages and warnings from your body. Just pay attention to the emotions being projected and you will have enough information to take corrective action.

It will help you if you have some idea of what spirits are sending you messages. Here are some of the categories we have identified: Spirits running individual cells, spirits running organs, spirits running nerve networks, spirits animating cancer cells and parasites and other opposing biological systems in the body.

There will also be messages from spirits merely residing in the body and not running any part of it. For example: Spirits who died from poisoning may take up residence in the stomach area. Spirits who died from body wounds may reside in that part of the body. When something happens to the body part they reside in, you will get all sorts of messages and painful images from their past experience.

If you use caring communication, you will be able to free the being or clusters of beings from the incident they are still stuck in and get them to leave or work with the rest of the body.

Sometimes beings are stuck in a struggle for survival from a past incident. They are still fighting a battle that was over centuries ago, but they are hanging on to their opponents to punish them. If you can get them to stop being adversaries, the body will heal and life will improve.

If you ignore a situation to the point where the pain or damage is overwhelming, you need to seek help from an experienced spiritual healer.

Do not ignore things you do not understand. Get help from someone you trust. A competent spiritual healer will also know when a situation requires medicine or surgery as well as spiritual healing. Do not try to heal with spirit alone when medical care is needed.

After medical care has been applied, make sure that all of the spiritual issues are carefully dealt with. Do not stop until the flow of life force has been restored.

The spirits running the body cells and organs
can be disturbed by physical causes
like poisons, or impact, or temperature,
but they will respond to direct communication
if you can locate and contact them with
caring communication.

The spirits located in the body
but not running it, are still affecting the body
when they get upset.
The pains and emotions they generate
can be felt by the host,
but can be handled completely
with caring communication.

INCREASE YOUR ABILITY TO COMMUNICATE WITH SPIRITS

Some of you are fortunate enough to be able to perceive spirits and communicate with them as soon as you know they exist. Little children often have this ability until well-meaning parents punish them for talking to their "imaginary" playmates.

Fortunately, there is a simple process that will enable almost anyone to rehabilitate their ability to perceive spirits and to know what they are thinking.

It is called Reach and Withdraw Processing and can be learned in a matter of hours, even as a do-it-yourself project.

When you master this process, you will be able to communicate with almost any spirit and be able to understand his motives and his intentions.

Reaching and withdrawing is done spiritually by putting your attention on something or someone and then withdrawing your attention from it until you can assume the viewpoint and intentions of the target.

This process has removed antagonism between people, increased psychic abilities, enabled people to live more fearlessly, and increased empathy to a remarkable degree.

REACH AND WITHDRAW PROCESSING

One of the major results from the completion of this process is that the person running the process becomes cause over their relationship with the target. The target can be a person, a spirit, an organization, a location, a feeling, or a craving.

There are other, more significant results from running this process and you are encouraged to discover them at your leisure.

Reaching and withdrawing is done spiritually by putting your attention on something or someone and then withdrawing your attention from it until you can assume the viewpoint and intentions of the target.

The steps are done on a gradient until you are able to perceive what the other being is thinking about themselves and their lives.

The only prerequisite is that you must fully understand what caring communication is and how to do it.

The reach and withdraw process is done in three steps or until the objective is reached. Each step requires a higher level of confront so the person is led from a hesitant reach and withdraw to a full blown permeating of the target's space with the highest level of caring communication possible.

Here are the Reach and Withdraw commands in brief:

R1 - Reach for X, where X is any stuck flow, problem area, or person you cannot communicate with
W1 - Withdraw from X

R2 - Reach for X, using caring communication.
W2 - Withdraw from X and make sure all of your spiritual partners withdraw from X

R3 - Reach for X, using even more caring communication and permeate the space occupied by X.
Occupy X's viewpoint.
W3 - Withdraw from X and make sure you and all of your spiritual partners are completely disconnected from X

At some point in the process you will notice that the other being can perceive your presence, but this is not the end product of this process.

Repeat reaching and withdrawing until you have a major realization and feel good about reaching into the other being's space.

In every session I have run, the person doing the process has grimaced and flinched in the beginning and had physical reactions while reaching and has originated realizations while withdrawing.

If a spiritual being wakes up and demands you address their concern, handle them with the usual Talking To Spirits process.

You are welcome to experiment with further alterations if you feel that it will make it easier to run reach and withdraw on a difficult target.

The action of reaching and withdrawing is an essential step in any effective communication. When you can confidently occupy someone else's space, you can communicate to them without harming them or scaring them. You will see that you can understand the person's needs and their intentions and will be able to communicate effectively with them in a caring way.

When you practice reaching and withdrawing effectively, you also become cause over any beings who seek to block you from communicating. You will also find that you can do reach and withdraw on people and beings who are at a great distance from you. It is a worthwhile exercise of your psychic abilities and will pay great dividends.

It can also be done through physical movement to enable a person to operate something he is afraid of. Touching and letting go of a scary object will restore your ability to pick up and handle the object safely and effectively.

Effective communication with someone
requires duplication at both ends of the communication line.

If you can reach and withdraw freely
with respect to another being,
you are well on your way to "being"
that individuul and understanding
his needs and intentions.

Reach and withdraw until you truly know
the other beings you are dealing with and life will be simpler.

USING REACH AND WITHDRAW ON BODIES

Healing bodies requires a great deal of confront, and one of the best ways to develop an aptitude for healing body problems is to do Reach and Withdraw processing on the body, starting with your own.

Let's say you have an ache or pain in some part of your body, or your stomach does not feel well. Practice reach and withdraw on that part of your body until you feel confident you know what is going on and how to remedy the problem.

The first thing you may notice is that the body part will become warm and the problem area will start to disperse.

As you continue your reach and withdraw process, you will become aware of spirits who are opposed to what you are doing and are holding the problem in place.

You have a choice here, as you can continue reach and withdraw on the area including the beings as well until they relax and leave, or you can communicate directly with the beings who are creating the problem and handle whatever is causing them to create the problem.

After handling the beings who are creating the body problem, continue the reach and withdraw process until the body problem is completely solved.

Once you know how to handle a problem in your body, you might want to use your ability to help someone else handle a body problem.

You will also find that as your ability to reach and withdraw improves, you will be using this technique more frequently to monitor and control your body functions.

Your increased ability to put your attention on any area of your body will materially aid you in detecting problem areas and handling them before they become serious.

You should get better and better at controlling the life energy of your body so that your body stays healthy and recovers rapidly from any accidental damage. This may even improve your appearance because most of the signs of old age are actually signs of neglect.

When you stay on top of your physical and spiritual condition and eliminate unneeded stress from your life, your body will last longer without showing the usual signs of wear and tear.

YOU ARE MORE THAN YOUR BODY

It is important to remember that you are more than your body.

You will be around long after this body is gone and your mental health will be better served by being prepared for what you will be doing for your next lifetime and beyond.

Perhaps you should consider preparing for some long term goals that will keep you occupied for many centuries or eons.

You have many lifetimes and many more bodies to animate if you wish. Perhaps the best solution is to make every lifetime count. If you keep talking to spirits, you have the opportunity to create any future you wish.

Much more can be done with this knowledge. Once you become aware that you are immortal, and you can change your personality to fit the needs of any lifetime, you have the opportunity to make some outrageous long term plans.

WHAT KIND OF RESULTS CAN YOU EXPECT WHEN DEALING WITH SPIRITS?

If you understand what you are dealing with, you can achieve a dynamic stability where you can get predictable results from your interactions with the spirits surrounding you.

Your stable data are that spirits are basically helpful unless they are stuck in a past incident that is affecting their behavior.

You can free them from their past incidents and restore their free will by using caring communication.

The spirit world is constantly changing because spirits are usually in motion and they can come and go at will. You seek to communicate with a chosen spirit or group of spirits while other spirits listen in and comment and they will offer opinions and even express doubts about your abilities or the wisdom of talking to beings in an effort to help them.

If you know what you are trying to achieve, and that is beings freed from their past failures, you will be able to navigate your way through the complexities of a Talking to Spirits session.

Your interaction with spirits can be more easily understood if you have any familiarity with sailing.

In sailing, you are making a boat proceed from a departure point to a destination point over a completely unstable supporting medium by capturing wind that varies in force and direction and using it to propel your craft in a desired direction.

The boat is never stable, but it is maintained in a state of dynamic stability by altering the shape and position of sails and by redistributing the weight of the crew to keep the boat from taking on water and sinking.

The goal is reached by constantly adjusting the sails, rudder, and balance of the ship to take advantage of the prevailing winds and the tide. The course is not a straight line, it is the course of the least resistance, keeping in mind the final destination.

When you deal with spirits, you are communicating with living thoughts and you are doing this while immersed in a veritable carnival of spiritual activity.

You work with a set of chosen spirits, but you must remain aware of unseen spiritual activity in the background.

For example, a new client can experience a session where a long term problem with his brother is handled by sorting out a fierce battle between ancient clans, where the battle of the clans has been going on for thousands of years.

Viewpoints change when he discovers that he and his brother have spiritual companions from different clans and that is where their life long antagonism comes from.

The client will experience great relief in the session and then as the session ends, he will get the strange feeling that it was all a made up story that the counselor pushed on him. He will even get the feeling that this is what you get when you mess with spiritual things! Fake memories!

The experienced counselor merely nods and asks where the feeling of falseness is coming from and gets the client to spot the beings who are unable to experience relief because of their own failed efforts to help others. These beings act as hecklers when you are trying to conduct a session and are a distraction.

Since you are reading this book and doing sessions on your own, you will experience many of the doubts and uncertainties that my clients have been experiencing for years, until they spotted where the doubts were coming from.

You will resolve these feelings of doubt and uncertainty when you read the next section, SPIRITS YOU CANNOT HANDLE ALONE

When you finally realize that most of the negative thoughts you have been experiencing for years are not your own, you will run sessions faster and more confidently than before.

You will also be able to accept that the beings you are talking to can suddenly wake up and vanish before the sessions steps are complete.

You will also accept that other beings can barge into the session and demand to be handled immediately. You may also be able to perceive that other beings may be influencing the being you are communicating with.

If you hold to the stable data that we are freeing beings from ancient incidents of great emotional pain, shame, and regret, you will be able to experience anything that happens in the session and be confident that peace will eventually prevail.

With experience, you will recognize when a troublesome spirit or spirits have moved off and will know to end off any session activity in that regard.

You will also recognize when you have picked up new spirits with similar problems to what you have handled previously, and will not invalidate your earlier handlings. There will be more than one group of spirits with problems of insecurity or betrayal, for example, and it may take multiple sessions before all have been awakened and handled.

You will eventually realize that with each group of spirits handled and acknowledged, your own psychic powers are revitalized and that your ability to look at an individual or group and predict behavior has expanded.

You will know what people are going to say before they say it and somehow you will find that you have become happier and that life has become more enjoyable.

You will know that life will bring constant change, but you will be ready for it and will happily look forward to the future.

When you deal with spirits,
you are using telepathy
to communicate with them
and this process cannot be captured
by conventional senses and devices
and you are doing this while immersed
in a veritable carnival of spiritual activity.

If you hold to the stable data that we are freeing beings
from ancient incidents of great emotional pain,
shame, and regret,
you will be able to experience anything
that happens in the session
and be confident that peace will eventually prevail.

You will eventually realize
that with each group of spirits you handle,
your own psychic powers are revitalized
and your ability to predict behavior has expanded.

A FRANK CHAT ABOUT GENDER UNCERTAINTIES

1. A Spirit Is Sexless

Once you really understand the complicated relationship between spirits and bodies, you will find that you have a more relaxed view of people who seem to have urges at variance with their body type. You will also have a true understanding of those people of one sex who identify as a member of the opposite sex. All of the data in this article comes from hundreds of spiritual counseling session hours.

The urges toward sexual activity and sexual attraction are spiritual in nature and can easily be understood once you realize that a spirit has no sex or sexual parts, but generally has a history of operating successfully in a male or female body.

For the rest of this article, I will call these spirits with a successful history in bodies of a particular sex "male spirits" or "female spirits".

2. A Spirit Will Have a Sexual History If He Has Owned Bodies

If a being has operated as a male successfully for many lifetimes and happens to pick up a female body in a moment of excitement or inattention, this "male spirit" may run the female body in a way that emphasizes masculine qualities and may not ever develop a true femininity.

Talking to the spirit will not change his sexual orientation, but will make his life as a woman with masculine urges more comfortable.

138

On the other hand, if a being has operated as a female successfully for many lifetimes and happens to pick up a male body, this "female spirit" may run the male body in a way that emphasizes feminine qualities and may not ever develop a true masculinity.

Talking to the spirit will not change her sexual orientation, but will make her life as a man with feminine urges more comfortable.

Between these two extremes, there are a number of different situations depending on the number of spirits surrounding the body with different gender preferences. These can be helped significantly with Talking to Spirits processing.

3. Talking To Spirits Processing
A normally masculine male (male spirit in a male body) with enough "female spirits" around him will find that he is attracted to male bodies in a way that he does not consider manly and he is right.

His "female spirit" companions are attracted to males and will draw his attention to male bodies and may even arouse him with respect to male bodies.

Spiritual counseling can handle these "female spirits" and get them to leave or work with the male spirit in a less distracting way. When spirits are brought into present time, they usually are able to work in harmony with the spirit running the body regardless of their sexual orientation. They become team members and contribute to the goals of the group.

A normally feminine (female spirit in a female body) with enough "male spirits" around her will find that she is attracted to female bodies in a way she does not consider proper and she is right.

Her "male spirit" companions are attracted to females and will draw her attention to female bodies and may even arouse her with respect to female bodies.

Spiritual counseling can handle these "male spirits" and get them to leave or work with the female spirit in a less distracting way.

When spirits are brought into present time, they usually are able to work in harmony with the spirit running the body regardless of their sexual orientation. They become team members and contribute to the goals of the group.

This point is important enough to merit repeating it.

When spirits are brought into present time, they usually are able to work in harmony with the spirit running the body regardless of their sexual orientation. They become team members and contribute to the goals of the group.

4. Spirits With No Preference About Sexual Orientation

We also encounter spirits who have run both male and female bodies for a long period of time and who have no real preference for what gender bodies they occupy. They can freely exhibit both male and female characteristics but they can suffer from not understanding or agreeing with what society expects of them.

Spiritual counseling gives them an understanding of their true situation and will also handle any confusions of the "male" and "female" spirits surrounding this non-preferential being.

Once a spiritual being understands why it has certain urges and behaviors, it can freely choose to associate with beings with the same spiritual condition or to associate with anyone without feeling guilty for being different.

Gender uncertainty is not catching, but the spiritual uncertainty may be buried for many years until some event triggers the realization that something is wrong about the role the person has been playing. This realization can happen at any time and initiates a period of stress which may continue for the rest of the person's life. Spiritual counseling can ease the person into understanding who they really are and how this situation occurred.

Knowing who you really are and why you act the way you do will give you the certainty you need to live fearlessly.

Once a spiritual being understands why it has certain urges and behaviors, it can freely choose to associate with beings with the same spiritual condition or to associate with anyone else without feeling guilty for being different.

141

5. Body Modification

Some people have decided that they want to modify their bodies to match their spiritual orientation, but this has not always been successful and some have regretted their decision to change their physical gender.

Physical modification without understanding the spiritual implications will have unexpected results. Counseling will help but unless the counseling truly handles the spirits involved, spiritual problems may make life a real challenge.

If you are one who is comfortable in your gender role, this article may make it easier to understand those who have gender confusions and give you a viewpoint that enables you to help them.

If someone says they identify as a member of a different sex, they are probably on the right track.

Urges toward sexual activity and sexual attraction
are spiritual in nature and can easily be understood
once you realize that a spirit has no sex or sexual parts
but generally has a history
of operating successfully in a male or female body.

Knowing who you really are
and why you act the way you do
will give you the certainty you need
to live comfortably in your
gender role.

SPIRITS CONSTANTLY AFFECT YOUR BEHAVIOR, HEALTH, AND PERSONALITY

Constantly is the operative word. It means that spirits are affecting you 24/7 whether you are awake or dreaming.

When your spirits are happy, they cheer you up and can help you achieve great things with very little effort..

When they get triggered, they can bring you down, sometimes all the way to despair. They can change with no warning and you can go from feeling great to feeling sick and tired in a matter of minutes.

When you have your spiritual team in good shape, they will pick up on incoming threats and you will not be blindsided as long as you listen to their warnings.

You do not have to be responsible for external events, but you can be responsible for your reaction to them.

This means what it says: spirits constantly affect your behavior, health, and personality.

See my numbered comments below:

1. Spirits surround you at all times. They may have been with you for centuries or longer or you may have picked them up at the funeral home you just visited to pay respects to a departed friend. They may even be the spirits of your dead spouse or parents who still feel they have to look after you.

2. Constantly means what you think it means. There is never a moment that you are not affected by the spirits who surround you. If you can harness their abilities, you will operate at a very high level. If you are fighting your spirits, life can be very difficult.

3. Affect means everything from influencing you in a slight way to actually taking control of your body and acting in ways you cannot control. This happens more often than you might think.

4. Behavior includes your tendency to comment on things that you hear without thinking. It includes the mannerisms like picking at scabs, biting your nails, and fiddling with your hair. It includes your irritability at kids screaming, slow drivers in front of you, and the idiots who make stupid comments on Facebook.

It also includes your inability to speak up to the boss when he treats you like a serf and your inability to speak in front to large groups. Spirit-controlled behavior includes your craving for alcohol every day, or cigarettes, or even chocolate donuts.

Spirits can cause you to do positive things like filling your house with flowers every day or running marathons or attending rock concerts. Their ability to influence our choices in life has to be fully examined to realize how much of what you do every day is influenced by the spirits who are trying to help you.

5. Health means everything related to the operation of your body. Your health is constantly being affected by your spirits. You will not have any subjective reality on this until you see a painful physical condition vanish on the completion of a Talking to Spirits session.

6. Personality is the entire package of attitudes, behaviors, beliefs, motivations, in short all of the characteristics you exhibit that people recognize you by.

Now you can either decide to be the effect of all these spirits, or you can decide to manage them for your benefit. Talking To Spirits as described in this book has all of the tools you will need to help your spirits contribute to your welfare or to set them free to create independent lives of their own.

The spirits who surround you can be a resource or a nightmare depending on how you treat them.

If you foolishly try to get rid of the spirits who surround you, you might end up like too many Scientologists who have tried this, sick and miserable due to the counter intentions of unhappy spiritual beings. Spirits do not like being scraped off.

Any spiritual practice that resembles exorcism will produce unhappy and resentful spirits who will basically haunt you with counter-intentions to everything you try to accomplish. This will act as a self-inflicted curse which will not lift until you get into caring communication with the spiritual beings who have been driven off by the exorcism.

Some spiritual practices are closer to exorcisms than conversations and can produce unwanted results because of the spirits who are upset by the process. Any counseling process that tries to modify behavior runs the risk of alienating spirits who are trying to help and this leads to upset spirits.

Talking To Spirits will give you the tools you need to create a better existence for you and for your spiritual companions.

When a being takes responsibility for an action
he becomes cause over the results of that action.

Almost all spiritual problems you will encounter
are a result of trying to avoid responsibility
for something that was done.

In many cases
the result of an unplanned action
was so unexpected and horrific
the spiritual being could not confront
the idea that he was responsible for the result.

He will be trapped in that confusion
until you seek him out and talk to him in a caring way,
and get him to acknowledge his responsibility,
at which point he will be freed.

HOW DO YOU ENCOURAGE SPIRITS TO HELP YOU?

First of all, are you really willing to let spirits assist you in everyday life? If you are comfortable with the idea of having a team of helpful spirits at your beck and call, you will have no trouble persuading spirits to help you with things they consider interesting.

On the other hand, if you consider your life to be boring and you are not very happy with who you are, you may not attract many helpful spirits. You may have too many troubled spiritual companions messing up your environment.

I suggest that you ask every spirit you talk to if they would like to join your team and work with you. The ones who join may need some suggestions on what they can do for you. Usually you will be able to tell from what they have been doing in previous lifetimes.

If you give the being an assignment, he will often join in with no difficulty. On the other hand, he may wander off if you are not doing anything challenging or entertaining.

I have found that working with spirits daily on challenging tasks will keep them interested and productive. Frequently acknowledging them for their contributions is vital as this is the major exchange we can provide to them.

They are not servants or automatons. They are beings like yourself with a long history of work experience which you can tap into if you are polite and give them credit for their contributions.

One of the best ways I found to manage them in the beginning, was to hold frequent staff meetings with my spiritual companions in which we discussed ongoing projects. These staff meetings eventually give way to ongoing conversations on the topic or project at hand.

When you have a group that is telepathically connected, there is little need for meetings or memos. You do need communication discipline so that beings stay on topic when necessary.

In addition, I run informal meetings every morning as I wake up to see what the team wants to share with me. The morning meeting is unstructured and covers whatever they want to communicate to me.

I will get suggestions on all sorts of matters, from bills to pay, to articles to write, even people I should follow up on. Most interesting are the solutions they present for long standing problems.

If I encounter a problem and they have useful data which might resolve it, I get immediate input and resolve the problem on the spot. On the other hand, there are times when several solutions are presented with no clear winner. A few days or weeks will go by and someone will present a solution that works.

CHALLENGES OF WORKING WITH EAGER TEAMMATES

Once you accumulate a group of beings who want to help you and who are participating in many important events of your daily life, your challenges may just be starting.

For example, once you realize how useful some of your spiritual partners can be, you will start relying on them to assist you without micromanaging them. They will make your life so much easier that you can lose sight of the fact that they are creating effects that you are not noticing. You may only be aware that you are getting things done with very little effort or attention.

Unless you keep your eye on what effects are being created when you use these teammates, you will find yourself communicating in ways that produce negative results. You can even undo some of the goodwill you have created previously.

There is a subtle trap that occurs when you knowingly use spiritual teammates to assist you in accomplishing challenging tasks. Everything seems to become easier and your attention goes on to the fact you are accomplishing difficult activities with very little effort or attention.

The problem is especially damaging if the activity is a real time activity like public speaking or counseling, because the action can include inputs from spiritual teammates that will occur before you have time to anticipate or analyze them.

These unexpected inputs can include profanity, jokes, non sequitur remarks to make a point, and attitudes which transform a conversation into a boring rant.

I have been spotting some of these recently and have handled the spiritual beings responsible for the unwanted inputs. The jokes, non sequitur remarks, and the profanity have been addressed and are no longer a problem. My teammates were merely trying to spice up my conversation and keep the audiences attention.

I also had a being named Ernest who was helping me communicate the importance of communicating with spirits. His contributions were significant, but had the unfortunate result of transforming almost any communication into a boring rant. His story follows.

Working With Ernest
Observing that my articles were becoming boring rants has been a persisting problem and was only resolved when I discovered Ernest, my resident pedant.

With the help of Kathy Elliott, I located Ernest who was a pedantic educator. His mission in life has been to make sure that people REALLY got the importance of understanding and communicating with spirits.

He is VERY SERIOUS about this and this attitude will restimulate you and your spirits and put you all to sleep almost instantly. He is still wearing his black academic robes.

Ernest says: (*The origins of academic dress date back to the 12th and 13th centuries, when universities were taking form. The ordinary dress of the scholar, whether student or teacher, was the dress of a cleric.*)

Ernest has a tremendous grasp of facts and has used his knowledge to mold generations of young scholars into reasonably well-trained professionals. He has always had a captive audience and never had to attract and retain clients as I have.

His strength was in his depth of knowledge and his rigor in the matter of instruction. He would not stop until the student had grasped the material or had fled.

Unlike Richard Feynman, Ernest never saw the need for humor in his instruction of others and did not ever see instruction as entertainment.

It appeared to me that unless one had an unquenchable thirst for knowledge, one would have a difficult time learning from Ernest. His uncompromising attitude toward exactness will put almost anyone into a state of unconsciousness.

Ernest is still with me and lends rigor to my writing, but he is now operating in present time and has accustomed himself to the needs of online writing and readers who have other places to be if we do not entertain them.

He has a huge vocabulary and every so often I find myself wanting to use a word that I have never used before but is exactly right for a particular purpose. To keep myself honest, I look up the word before committing it to the internet.

Ask every spirit you talk to
if they would like to join your team
and work with you.

Usually you can tell what they can do for you
from what they have been doing in previous lifetimes.

If you give the being an assignment,
he will often join in with no difficulty.
But he may wander off if you are not doing anything
challenging or entertaining.

I have found that working with them daily
on challenging tasks will keep them interested
and productive.

Frequently acknowledging them
for their contributions is vital
as this is the major exchange
we can provide to them.

SOME GUIDELINES FOR GETTING EFFECTIVE HELP

When you possess a self-aware group of spiritual companions, you can acquaint them with the ideal scene you wish to create and they will reorganize themselves so you present a personality to the world that will enable you to achieve your ideal scene.

If you support your spiritual partners by giving them instructions and drilling them on getting the results you want on the proper gradient, you will find that getting results is almost magical.

Here are monitoring functions you might want your team to establish: indicators like emotional tone level, energy level, health, income, bank balances, the emotional state of your environment, and your ability to exercise free will.

You should establish an acceptable range for all of these indicators and when any indicator falls outside the acceptable range, the team should reorganize so that priority is given to those spiritual teammates who can address the issue and resolve any difficulty.

Any indicator can be a signal to take action, but the leading indicators are your emotional tone level and your energy level. Any fluctuation in either of these will result in a similar change in the lagging indicators of health, income, friendly/unfriendly comm and free will.

A long term drop in emotional tone level or energy level is an extreme danger signal and a well-drilled team should be trained to identify and help handle the probable causes by shifting roles and responsibilities to address the problem areas.

If the indicators do not lift after the team reorganizes, a fresh assessment needs to be done and an emergency reorganization must occur under your direction that will change conditions permanently.

If the situation remains untenable after you have taken all reasonable actions, the group must be prepared to relocate to a less hostile environment. If you and your group are unable to change the state of an environment, you need to change to a new environment where your efforts will be rewarded.

If you find that you are running into the same problems in the new environment, get counseling to see what necessary attributes you are missing. Some of your spiritual companions may need repair or replacement.

CREATING THE FUTURE YOU WANT

A recent workshop on creating a desirable future made me realize that a well drilled team of spiritual teammates can anticipate and effectively respond to intolerable situations without changing management personnel.

This requires that the team be self aware and recognize itself as a team with members having specific abilities and personalities along the lines of: intuition, reason, analytical ability, insight, organizing ability, ability to focus, compassion, ability to define creative solutions to problems, and ability to execute flawlessly to produce a given result.

There are a host of other desirable attributes your spiritual partners can have including the ability to charm, entertain, to deliver sparkling repartee, and convince others of important matters, but there is a definite subset of abilities that will enable you to escape from intolerable situations or avoid them altogether.

An intolerable situation will drain your life force and leave you unhappy and in ill health. Your spiritual teammates have solutions for you if you can listen to them. Your spiritual teammates are very aware of the stresses caused by your work or relationships and will generally have reasonable suggestions for you if you pay attention to them.

There is another way in which your teammates can help. You may be helping people in a number of areas that are not related to production of income or emotional support.

If you are spreading your life energy over areas not related to production of needed results, that can be holding you back from success. Try focusing your attention and life energy on the areas of life that you want to flourish and prosper.

Ask your teammates in solo sessions if they have suggestions for directing your energies for better results. You may be surprised at what they have to say. Using your spiritual teammates as trusted advisors keeps them on their toes and shows that you value their contributions.

*You may be helping people in a number of areas
that are not related to production of income
or emotional support.*

*If you are spreading your life energy over areas
not related to production of needed results,
that can be holding you back from success.*

*You need to be able to recognize situations
that will drain your life force and leave you unhappy
and in ill health.*

*Try focusing your attention and life energy
on the areas of life
that will help you flourish and prosper.*

A Possible Guide To The Benefits to be Gained From Working with Your Spirits

Your Life With Spiritual Rescue Technology
Use the material below to change your life for the better

This is where you live fearlessly and joyfully create your life every day with total certainty that you are doing what you want to do and that it benefits every life that you touch. This is a good place to be, and you can get here by starting at the bottom and doing the steps shown.

What You Do	Spiritual Activity	What You Receive
Merely ask the right questions of your spiritual companions	**Access to Spiritual Knowledge**	Knowledge about anything that has ever been done
Find beings who are helping and help them to be more effective	**Working With Spirits**	Extraordinary level of support in all activities so you get things done with almost no effort
Locate upset beings who are stuck in old incidents and you set them free to create new lives	**Rescuing Spirits**	Incredible relief from the upsets and guilt your spirits have been carrying around for years
Use Caring Communication to engage with the beings who impinge upon your awareness	**Talking to Spirits**	You discover an entire realm of new possibilities and gain hope that you can change your life for the better
You are desperate enough to see some change in your life	You search the Internet for Spiritual Rescue Technology	You find a way to do things you have never done before

This is your starting point where you struggle to overcome barriers in a seemingly insane world. This is life as a normal human being who is concerned about their mortality. You can move out of this position by doing the steps outlined above.

If you have any questions, contact David St Lawrence - srtcounseling@gmail.com

Spirits You Cannot Handle Alone

In this section you will learn about the beings you will need help to handle. These are the beings responsible for spiritual possession, walk-ins, curses, dementia and other manifestations of being under someone else's control. We will also cover hypnotic implants and other mind control incidents.

The existence of these spiritual incidents can be detected by someone who is extremely aware, but the handling of these incidents will almost always require help from another trained person. All of these situations can be handled and have been successfully handled with talking to spirits processing performed by a trained spiritual counselor.

The reason that you will almost always require help is that the beings described in this section may actively interfere with you when you seek to handle them. Most of them think they are in charge and will take control of the session as soon as it starts. These are the spirits who can control you as opposed to spirits who can only influence you.

It is important that you read and understand the material in this part of the book, because these are the most capable beings you will encounter. If you use caring communication on them, you may find common interests with them and get them to join your team of spiritual companions as working members of the team.

If these spirits have goals and interests that are aligned with your own, they can be incredibly helpful in every part of your professional and personal life.

If their interests and yours are not aligned, you need to be able to get them pointed in another direction where their talents can be better utilized.

Having unaligned spiritual companions is a continual distraction.

Any time you have beings in your space who are not enthusiastic about what you are doing, you will have their counter-intention acting against your intention to succeed. The absence of their negativity will make it easier to accomplish things. Once they leave, you will experience relief and will be able to accomplish more than when they were present.

After reading this section, if you suspect that you are being affected by any of the beings described in this part of the book, feel free to contact me for advice.

David St Lawrence
540-320-6852
srtcounseling@gmail.com

The beings described in this section
are the most capable beings you will encounter.

You will need help to handle them
because these spiritual beings
may actively interfere with you when you seek to help them.

These are the spirits who can control you
as opposed to spirits who can only influence you.

These beings will resist being discovered
and will make it difficult
to read and understand this book.

If you would like a free check to see if you have
beings who do not want you to talk to spirits
and are stopping you from reading this book
and going free, call or text me.

David St Lawrence
540-320-6852
srtcounseling@gmail.com

DETECTING BEINGS YOU CANNOT HANDLE BY YOURSELF

When you become proficient at talking to spirits and releasing them from the traps they devised for themselves, do not be surprised if you encounter spiritual beings that you cannot handle by yourself. I do not want you to take a loss if you encounter any of these beings, so I will first give you some advice on how to detect one when it appears.

You will not be able to handle any of these beings by yourself, unless you are desperate and very determined. You will need help to handle them because these spiritual beings will actively interfere with your efforts to detect and handle them.

Fortunately, you will be able to detect the presence of these beings if you are prepared and know what to look for.

There are several groups of beings who cannot be handled in a solo session.

1. Beings who make you go unconscious.
2. Spirits who take control of your actions
3. Beings who distract you and keep you off balance so you cannot carry out needed activities.
4. Beings whose crimes are unconfrontable
5. Beings who think they are you
6. Walk-ins and permanent possession by another spirit

There are definite signs if one of the above identified beings is affecting you. The signs of their presence are numbered accordingly.

1. Beings who make you go unconscious

You keep yawning and nodding off when you attempt to contact this type of being. This can escalate to the point where you actually go unconscious when someone asks you about a topic which triggers the being's incident.

This being is carrying an enormous burden of unconsciousness from an incident where he lost his life.
He has been unable to shed the confusion and blame he carries for what happened.

You may find that both you and your counselor may briefly go unconscious while you are attempting to handle the being in a session.

2. Spirits who take control of your actions

If you encounter a being who takes control of your actions, you will not have a clear memory of what is happening. You will become upset at your counselor because he does not seem to understand you and is not asking the right questions.

You will feel grumpy during the session and will not know why. It will seem like the counselor is not listening to you because he is not agreeing with you and helping you to get better.

For some reason, you will not be able to get a name for this being and you will attempt to avoid answering the counselors questions.

If the counselor is persistent enough to discover the being who is doing this, you may experience disorientation and want to discontinue the session.

If the counselor is gentle and uses caring communication, the being who is running you may wake up, and you and the being may have a moment of clarity when you both realize what happened to him to put him in his current state.

If you are fortunate enough to have a counselor who can free you from this being, you will realize that you have not been yourself for most of your life. You have been under the control of a being who has been hiding out in an effort to survive and avoid discovery. You will both feel better when he wakes up and comes to present time.

3. Beings who distract you and keep you off balance so you cannot carry out needed activities.
If you have some of these beings around you, it will be almost impossible to carry out any protracted effort to improve yourself.

These beings keep you distracted and off balance so you cannot carry out helpful activities. I do not believe that this is a deliberate activity, it is more a continuous franticness where the being's attention shifts from one topic to another as soon as you put attention on analyzing what is going on.

You can tell when you have some of these beings affecting you in life because you will be unable to complete tasks lasting more than a few minutes. If you start to pick up your office, for example, after an attempt to organize some documents, you will find yourself on your smartphone scanning your calendar and browsing Facebook.

When you pull yourself together and look at your desk again, you will find several bills that must be paid immediately as soon as you can find where you left your checkbook.

You will not be able to find your checkbook because you left it in the car and you will decide to find it later and get lunch instead.

Almost everyone has beings like this around them and yet when getting a counseling session, this problem is the last to be mentioned. Beings of this type make your attention skitter from topic to topic and the unwary counselor can overlook the skittering and go for the topics uncovered.

Handling this type of being will restore calm to your life and will make you so much more productive that you will look back and be amazed at the confusion you have escaped.

4. Beings whose crimes are unconfrontable

There are times when you suddenly have a terrifying certainty that you are guilty of some obscenely awful act, but cannot seem to identify what it was. This certainty can be emphasized by the appearance of multiple disgusting dream sequences that are very real and leave you shaking.

The appalling thing about this type of incident is that you feel the emotion of self-disgust and terror, but you cannot seem to justify how or why you got into this terrible situation.

You will experience the guilt and horror, but you cannot seem to figure out how it happened.

If this happens to you, you have woken up a being who is desperately trying to escape a horror in his past and you are getting the benefit of his fear and self-loathing and thinking they are your own feelings.

Call a spiritual counselor and lay this tortured being to rest. You will all feel better when his incident is handled.

5. Beings who think they are you

There will be days when you do not act like yourself and cannot seem to snap out of this unhappy frame of mind. This is usually accompanied by mood swings you cannot control even if you can see them coming on.

To others who know you, it will seem as if you have an invisible co-pilot who takes over when things do not go your way. You may even be dimly aware that you turn on this alternate personality at times but you have no control over the transition.

The transition can be short-lived, lasting only seconds, or it can last for days or even months depending on the stimulus. The transition can be dramatic or subtle, but you are not the same person when the transition occurs and the effects on your life and your relationships can be permanent.

Even when you are aware you are going into an altered state, you are unable to observe and analyze what is going on. You have a being or several beings who assume command when something in the environment triggers the switch.

A competent spiritual counselor will be able to discover the reason for the multiple personalities struggling for control and will enable all beings to reach agreement on a new arrangement.

6. Walk-ins - permanent possession by another spirit

Unfortunately, if you are the walk-in, you will not be able to detect this condition by yourself, as you may not remember who was in charge before you arrived. You may discover this if someone mentions that you sure have changed since your operation or since the accident that almost killed you.

If you suspect that you are a walk-in, try remembering images from early parts of your life. You just may find that the early images are all still pictures while more recent images are available as full motion videos.

If you have encountered any of these situations, you need to pull in reinforcements. A trained spiritual counselor is the best solution, but a perceptive friend who cares for you may be all that you have at hand.

Knowing that you are being possessed by beings as described above may give you enough certainty to manage yourself and stay out of trouble until you find someone who can help.

The biggest problem these beings present is that they are the most intelligent and aggressive beings I have encountered in session. In some cases they are more able than you are.

You will find help if you can describe the problem to your potential reinforcement. Use the data in this chapter to show them what is happening. A trained spiritual counselor should be able to give you lasting relief.

If you have gotten this far and are still uncertain about the fanciful idea of being controlled by spirits, you are not alone. Some of the more prominent names in the spiritual counseling game are not aware that they are being controlled by spirits.

I will give you one final clue.

Those people who are being controlled by spirits will have fixed ideas about the roles that women and men should play in society and they strongly resist the idea that our personality aspects are separate beings.

*If you are completely certain
that you are in control of your life at all times,
You are probably under the control of another being.*

*Since the beings described in this section
are the most capable beings you will ever encounter,
you may well be happy with what they are doing.*

*If you feel you are in control
and are still unhappy with your life,
you may wish to change your goals.*

*At that point,
you will probably see resistance to your new goals.
Contact a trained counselor and get help.*

A SESSION EXAMPLE OF SPIRITS WHO MAKE YOU GO UNCONSCIOUS

We encountered a situation that I had not seen before, a cluster of spiritual beings that took two of us to handle. The client has been aware for some time that something was wrong but he was unable to locate it or to begin handling it on a solo basis.

Basically, it appeared to be similar to the distraction strategy executed by some spirits which we have all experienced. We start something and our attention is smoothly diverted to something else and we switch course and continue with the new effort and completely lose sight of the original action.

This was a cluster of beings who used a completely different strategy which made it extremely difficult to spot. When the client would start something that triggered a response, the group would go into hiding and the client would go unconscious for a short period of time.

When consciousness returned, the client could not remember what he was doing and he would have to start over. You could say the spirits "went elsewhere" and suppressed the client's awareness at the same time.

We had a difficult time communicating with the cluster even after we located it. It did not provide any information and did not even seem to have a personality. It was almost like one of those animals which drop and "play dead" as soon as they are detected.

Asking the client questions was a challenge because his attention would get hijacked as soon as he received the question.

By discussing the "going unconscious" action with me each time it occurred, the client was soon able to spot when it was going to occur and started getting information from the cluster. The client's persistence was admirable and he did everything possible to show the spirits that he was there to help them.

After a while they started to tell him their story.

The story involved a population that was destroyed in a massive explosion and then was captured and implanted and then put on display as "trophies". Their solution to the humiliation was to go "elsewhere" so the degradation would not affect them. That civilization was dust several universes ago, but this group of beings was holding the incident in place for themselves by going "elsewhere" when anything reminded them of this incident.

Even after describing the incident, the group was still stuck in the "unfairness" of it all because they were just peaceful citizens mowing lawns and gardening when WHAM, everything ended.

Since explosions and implants are motivators which occur after one has done something to upset someone else, we got them to look at what they had done to single themselves out as targets for destruction. Once we got what that was, the cluster broke up and quietly dispersed.

In short, this was just another cluster of beings stuck in an ancient incident which would get restimulated and cause the client trouble.

There are probably hundreds of them that you will encounter and handle with no difficulty. But, if they cause you to go unconscious like this one did, you will probably need help in handling them.

SESSION EXAMPLES OF SPIRITS WHO TAKE CONTROL OF YOUR ACTIONS

There are spirits who take control of your actions for a period of time and you are powerless to prevent this from happening.

If you are one of the unfortunates in this situation, you may be able to spot when it happens, but for most who are afflicted in this way you will not have a clue when it occurs.

Your only feedback will be from friends and loved ones who will tell you that you are acting in ways that do not agree with what you remember doing. This will be hard to accept because your version of what occurred will not agree with their version.

This is an example of temporary possession by another spirit and it is far more common than you might realize.

When the being takes over, you will be pushed into the background and will have no memory of the event. It is equivalent to being made unconscious for the interval when the other spirit takes control.

This form of possession is intermittent, and when you are not possessed, you will revert to your normal personality.

1. The Evil Twin Personality
Parents observe this in children and comment on the existence of an "evil twin" personality. They are more correct than they realize.

This form of possession can occur when two or more beings seek to pick up the same body at birth and nobody relinquishes their claim on the body. Usually, the beings negotiate an uneasy truce where one spirit runs the body most of the time and the other spirits occasionally take control when something occurs to trigger the change.

Behavior modification therapy may get one personality to suppress itself, but the only lasting solution is to talk to the spirits involved and handle the basis for the original conflict.

Almost always the beings have a long standing feud that predates the struggle for possession of the body by millennia.

When you run into this in sessions you are delivering to others, you will realize that personal feuds have no time limit. If they are not handled by some intervention, these feuds can cause conflict for hundreds of thousands of years.

2. You Are Being Monitored

There are also situations where a being has been assigned to monitor you so that you will not regain your powers and wreak havoc on the world again. I usually find that the person or group who assigned the being as monitor no longer exists.

Getting the being to look at what that civilization is doing now always brings up images of a deserted planet or a planet in ruins. You can draw your own conclusions on how stable a totalitarian civilization is.

I get the being to tell me whether the agreement he made is still valid now that the other party no longer exists. The monitor realizes that he is no longer bound and leaves.

Once he is gone, the temporary possession vanishes and the person is free from spiritual control.

3. Triggered by the Mention of Politics
The most shocking instance of spirits who take control away from you is when you are discussing politics or religion.

Someone you know and like suggests that your choice of political candidate or religion shows a lack of understanding of the true nature of that person or religion. This infuriates you and you correct this person's ignorance on the matter. The person responds with an obviously biased report and you get exasperated at his refusal to accept the truth of your argument.

His calm reply goads you even further and you wonder how you could have been friends with this person for years and not noticed his character flaws. His refusal to be ashamed of his choices convinces you that there is no merit in continuing your relationship.

Unless someone is able to spot the being responsible for your upset and assist you in handling the real source of the being's upset, you will suffer the permanent loss of a relationship. Every time the person mentions the topic, it will trigger painful memories for your being who is still fixated on a situation he was never able to resolve.

If this has never happened to you, it may be hard to believe that it can also happen in a more minor situation like defining a word.

4. Triggered by the Use of a Word
I published an article using the word "axiom" which I defined to mean a self evident truth. A well-respected professional acquaintance wrote a comment saying that I was misusing the word.

I replied that I had defined what this word meant and I would continue to use the word as before.

This triggered a being who could not handle being challenged. In the space of several hours, this person's comments escalated to:

> "...You seem to have retained ******'s bitter conceit whenever anyone differs in opinion. It's not becoming...

> ...Why this obsession to attack friendly people?...

> ...I only challenged you on the meaning of a word and you relentlessly try to attack my persona, integrity and wisdom. You made this bitter vitriolic attack once before; it was disgraceful for a supposed wise man..."

My insistence on cheerfully ignoring his indignation had triggered a spiritual being who took control of this person's communication and made him say things I have never heard him say before.

I deleted his comments to remove any evidence of the being taking control of him on a public website and offered to give him a free session if he wished to locate the true cause of his upset.

Failing to handle this being can also threaten this person's professional future. He is a public figure and I am sure he will encounter other intellectual challenges from the public he is trying to reach. If an unknown definition of a word can set him off, others may take advantage of that reaction at an inopportune time.

Failure to handle beings who can take control of your life is a huge risk. Any sign of inability to control your temper or other urges should cause you to seek counseling.

Any sign of inability to control your temper or other urges should cause you to seek counseling.

*You have a being
who is capable of taking control of your actions
and this presents a huge risk
to your career and your future.*

*Failure to handle beings who can possess you
even temporarily is extremely dangerous.*

MORE SESSION EXAMPLES OF SPIRITS WHO TAKE CONTROL OF YOUR ACTIONS

This is an area that can be very difficult to confront, which is why I have included additional examples so you can see for yourself how insidious this can be and how difficult it can be to take action even when you see that it exists.

Just to give you the proper perspective, when a spirit takes control of your actions, you are not only not in control, you are oblivious to what is happening. It is as if you have been turned off and have been put elsewhere while the other being runs your body and your life.

1. He Who Would Not Be Named
A certain client would start a session in enthusiasm and some time during the session, his personality would change and he would make critical comments about the questions I was asking, saying they didn't apply, etc. When this occurred, his voice and attitude would change and his posture would become more aggressive.

This did not happen all the time, but as we had more sessions, it seemed to occur more often. When it was not happening, this client was extremely cooperative, very enthusiastic, and extremely excited about the possibilities of working with this spiritual technology.

As we handled more and more spirits who were acting as obstacles to the client's career, the client's emotional tone level and his confidence increased, but he would be subject to mood swings where he would become critical and at the end of the session would not seem to feel he had made any progress although he was voicing realizations excitedly during session.

I finally was able to perceive the existence of a being whose confidence and abilities were actually greater than the client at rest.

When the client was "himself", he was a friendly, self effacing young man who was aware of his many barriers to success. When this being took over, the personality underwent a major change and became confident and quite critical of all aspects of the counseling and of the other people studying this spiritual technology.

He was an extremely challenging being to communicate with because he never actually answered any of the process questions. He avoided identifying himself or how long he had been with the client. He was always awake and active, but he hid his presence well until I learned to spot his emotional signature which would appear when I asked questions that would require and honest and straightforward answer.

Once I learned to identify his presence and pressed him for details about himself, he became even more evasive and suggested that I had spirits who were suppressive and who needed to be removed. This was a source of amusement to my spiritual companions who had been present for thousands of successful counseling sessions.

I gave him one more session with the hope that I could establish communication with him and the client such that the client could become aware of what was going on. During this session I realized that this unnamed being was totally controlling the client such that the client had no recollection of what was going on in the session.

I told the client I could not help him under the current situation and returned his unused money.

I offered to take him back in session if he could manage to control his unnamed being. Unfortunately, he still has no idea of what I am talking about. He is being possessed by a being with greater abilities than himself.

This is the kind of situation that in the past has prompted the rise of exorcisms, which is a forcible extraction of spirits from a host. It can be done and has been done for centuries, but the results can cause spiritual damage to the host.

If I cannot get the host being to the point where he can regain control of his personality, I can at least leave the situation in a stable state. In this case, the unnamed spirit is not hostile to the host and is managing affairs to the best of his abilities.

The unnamed spirit gives every evidence of being in present time and is proceeding with his own agenda. This new agenda is causing the host and his spiritual entourage to continue a successful career with a more aggressive personality than usual, but only a close friend would notice. This client has no close friends, so his new personality will probably go unnoticed.

2. The Hidden Co-Pilot
This is the most difficult being to handle by yourself and will always require assistance from a trained spiritual counselor.

This individual is always awake and seems to act as a hidden co-pilot. He will take over immediately whenever he feels threatened with exposure. He will have a different value system from yours and may cause you to say or do things that are destructive to others.

In most cases, he will prevent you from doing sessions on spirits because he wants to limit the exercise of free will by others.

His reaction to sessions is almost always negative, although the objections will not appear to be direct refusal. His usual approach will be to insist that the commands are incorrect, that the question has already been answered, and that nothing is wrong in the first place.

This being can be detected by others because of the change in your tone level he will create. If he allows you to start a session, you will find that he will overwhelm you with critical thoughts about what you are doing until you stop trying to talk and help spirits.

This hidden co-pilot will be fixed in a covertly hostile emotion so it will be very hard to spot what he is doing. He may even try to convince you he is doing this for your benefit, but the true test is that all of his efforts to help and advise you end badly.

If you work with a trained counselor, he will notice how rapidly your tone level will drops once the session starts and he will be able to handle the being and bring him to present time.

*If you are unable to benefit from skillfully
delivered spiritual counseling,
you are being controlled by beings
who are opposed to you exercising your free will
and going free.*

**When a spirit takes control of your actions,
you are not only not in control,
you are oblivious to what is happening.**

**It is as if you have been turned off
and have been put elsewhere
while the other being runs your body and your life.**

*Invariably, you will have difficulty
achieving gains in session
and if you do experience gains in a session
your enthusiasm will drop at the end of the session.*

*You should try to work with another counselor
and if the results are the same,
you are being controlled by beings
who are opposed to your becoming more able.*

*Failure to handle beings who can control you
is a huge liability and will affect your life adversely.*

*Your only solution is spiritual counseling
that incorporates Talking to Spirits techniques.*

SESSION EXAMPLES OF BEINGS WHO DISTRACT YOU AND KEEP YOU OFF BALANCE

Client: Independent Businessman - Difficulties As Mentioned:

Client was distracted when doing normal tasks.
This showed up when asking what his attention was on. His attention kept shifting from one topic to another. Client mentions he often talks to himself when he is doing things.

I asked client to do several things in sequence: move things, look at things, think of something. When client finished, I asked him if a voice was telling him to do each thing. Client could not remember.

Had client do several more actions in same way and notice whether a voice was repeating the actions. Client noticed that every action including thinking of something on command was accompanied by a voice.

Had client repeat with different actions and he was told to note where voice was coming from.

Client spotted a spiritual being behind his head and to his left. It was connected to a large cluster even further behind him. I had him cut the connection and we ran a session on the spirit by finding out what he was doing, when he had been assigned the task.

He had been assigned to monitor and harass the client and had been doing so for a very long time.

As usual, he had been forced into doing the task after having been found guilty for something he hadn't done so we pulled the string and found out what he had ignored that let him get betrayed. As soon as he spotted how he had compromised his own code of honor, he woke up and left.

Client was no longer distracted as much as before. He noticed that the voice effect was lessened also.

Reading comprehension is blocked.
Certain critical details that are important to the tasks at hand cannot be understood without rereading it again and again and there is great resistance to doing this.

(This was being caused by another being) We tackled the comprehension difficulty next. Client reads something fast and feels he has it but cannot remember it. After reading it several more times, he grasps it but then he loses the sense of it again. His particular difficulty was in interpreting a spreadsheet that ***he himself had created.***

I had him look for someone who was telling him he didn't need to read the spreadsheet or that it didn't matter. He soon spotted that a cluster of beings we had not yet handled was reacting to his efforts to read and understand the spreadsheet.

By making him confront the spreadsheet and try to read the spreadsheet while listening for responses, he picked up a sequence of comments and commands that disapproved of him using the spreadsheet.

This is typical behavior for spirits that are stuck in engrams (painful experiences). The client does something in his normal activities and that action triggers an spirit's engram so the client feels the spirit's emotion and thinks it is his own.

Once we spotted the cluster, we used spiritual processing to break up the cluster and bring the spirits to present time.

We found out what incident the cluster was stuck in and it had to do with something the client did a very long time ago. The cluster had been assigned to the client as a "security device" to track him and render him ineffectual so he would not commit other destructive actions.

We did the usual handling for clusters and spirits with infinitely long assigned tasks. We got them to look at why they were assigned to this thankless task, what had they done to deserve this assignment, whether there was still anyone left of the place they were, etc.

Once the group of spirits realized they had been sent off to get rid of them and the contract was invalid, they left.

The client immediately experienced a new willingness to read his spreadsheet. Since this was the reason for the session, we ended off at that point.

Almost everyone has beings who distract them.
This is such a universal condition that it has the become the
subject of jokes.

When someone finally does enough research
The remedy should be packaged and made readily accessible
in several different strengths tailored to specific situations.
for students, professionals, athletes, etc.

SESSION EXAMPLES OF BEINGS WHOSE CRIMES ARE UNCONFRONTABLE

Ever had the idea that you were Judas? The person responsible for the ultimate betrayal of Jesus Christ?

You are in good company because I have encountered two instances where some unfortunate individual was implanted (hypnotized) to think he was Judas.

Years ago in the late 1970s, when I was receiving auditing, I suddenly realized after one session that I had been Judas. There was no uncertainty about it. One moment, I was a happy go lucky seeker of truth and the next moment, I was absolutely certain I had been Judas. This struck me pretty hard and I resolved to avoid sharing this with anyone.

After a number of years, I came to grips with this knowledge and could speak of it to close friends who had discovered the seamier roles they had played in history. The only thing that kept puzzling me was that I had no mental image pictures of Jesus or of any disciples. All I had were still images of vacant scenery with olive trees.

Many years later during more advanced counseling, I realized that what I was feeling was a memory from a spiritual being who was accompanying me through life. At that point, the certainty of my identity as Judas blew and never troubled me again. I never was curious about how I had acquired this spirit and was happy that it had left.

Recently, in a spiritual counseling session a client originated that he had been Judas and we set about discovering whether this was his identity or an spirit's identity. It turned out that in a past life he had been killed by people he knew and had been implanted as he was dying in order to remove him as a factor at that critical point in history. The client had no personal knowledge of the person we call Jesus either.

One of the more interesting aspects of this particular session was the presence of off-planet forces which were determined to exert control over civilization at this time. So, not only was he supposedly responsible for a legendary betrayal, the incident involved alien forces as well. These two factors contributed to making the incident unconfrontable and difficult to resolve.

Now that the mystery of how he got to be "Judas" was resolved, he is free from the guilt he has been carrying for many many years.

So, if any of you readers have a similar burden to bear, get yourself a spiritual counseling session and sort out what really happened.

As an aside to this last example, I have encountered other accounts of alien activity during sessions covering that part of earth history. Most of the time, the aliens were trying to conceal their presence and we would only get a glimpse of what they were doing while we were resolving an incident for the beings we were helping.

The important result of a spiritual counseling session is the restoration of awareness and free will to the beings we are helping. Uncovering the hidden secrets of the universe is a minor benefit when it occurs. It should never overshadow freeing beings from the traps they have gotten themselves into.

The beings and situations you will encounter
may exceed your reality at first.

You will encounter beings
who have committed heinous actions
and consider themselves to be eternally damned.

If you try to handle these beings by yourself
it can be very hard to separate their memories
from your memories of these same actions.

Having someone else to keep you focused
on the process you are running
will allow you to resolve these incidents
of overwhelming guilt
and emerge free and clear of past memories.

If you and your counselor use caring communication
on the spirits you meet
you will achieve satisfying resolutions
to every situation.

SESSION EXAMPLES OF WALK-INS
AND PERMANENT POSSESSION BY OTHER
SPIRITS

If you were to carefully inspect the behavior of people returning home from major operations and injuries, you will detect the presence of other beings and some of them will have taken control of the body.

When someone's body is badly injured and unconscious for a long period of time, the original owner can get discouraged and leave, leaving the body to be controlled by a spirit looking for a new body. We call this newcomer a walk-in because he walks in when the original owner leaves.

When a person comes home from the hospital after his lengthy surgery and acts different and seems to have trouble with his memory, most people will blame his strangeness and lack of memory on the complications from his surgery and would not guess that someone else was running his body.

There are many reasons that a being will abdicate control of the body and turn control over to someone else. Here are a few:

> 1. A friend's wife came home from her fourth operation and she was not the same woman who went to the hospital. It was very hard on him as they had been very close and this was not the same being. This being was from a Third World culture and her personality did not resemble his wife's personality in any way.

2. I know people who discovered many years after the fact that they were walk-ins. They were getting counseling for something that happened to them as a child and they realized that they had taken possession of the body when it was very ill or injured.

3. I am a walk-in myself, having taken over this body when it was around 8 years old after it suffered heat stroke and was unconscious for 24 hours. The shift in ownership was particularly hard on my mother because I was not as obedient as the previous little boy. I challenged almost everything she said. I can still remember my father saying, "You never used to ask so many questions!"

4. I know a young person who was been possessed by multiple spirits after experiencing bullying at school. He basically stopped taking responsibility for his life and let any spirit in who sought keep him company.

After being institutionalized with no results, he received spiritual counseling and gradually learned how to take back control of his life.

He still is accompanied by spirits who keep him company and chat with him, but he is able to manage his life and continue his home schooled education. You might consider this an example of multiple walk-ins where no single spirit has total control.

There is no single solution for a walk-in or permanent possession of body by another being. Each situation needs to be addressed based on its own merits.

This is not a situation where an exorcism is called for or any remedial action at all.

The ideal resolution seems to occur when all of the facts are known, including the justifications for the change in control of the body. When all of the justifications are known, a mutually agreeable course of action is evident and there are no more issues to resolve.

Transferring control of a body
from one being to another
is not a matter to take lightly.

A trained spiritual counselor
can work with the beings involved
to make sure there are no loose ends to handle.

An ideal resolution can be reached
where life goes on under new management
and all outstanding issues are resolved.

SESSION EXAMPLE OF A SPIRITUAL BEING WHO THINKS HE IS "YOU"

This tends to show up when you ask when the spirit joined you. There will be an incident you both remember and you need to get all of the data and any decisions that were made at the time. You will also find that you will want to sort out different incidents in this or previous lifetimes when one of you was involved and the other wasn't.

You spot the spirit and are handling him when he originates he is "you" or he responds he is "you" when you ask his name. You merely continue running the process and get the details on the incident that he is fixated on. Do not be surprised if you find you were involved in the incident also. Just keep getting details on the incident and any points where the spiritual being compromised his personal integrity until he realizes who he actually is and is ready to create a new life for himself.

At some point, you will be able to separate out your individual experiences and will be able to spot the times you interacted while playing separate roles. Getting the original incident that bound you together will have the same effect as locating a cluster-making incident. The two of you made a decision that caused you to act as one from then on. Spotting that decision and the reason it was made will free you to act separately from now on.

There are at least two different situations when you will encounter a spiritual being who thinks he is you or is the being in charge of the body.

The first is the simplest and is the situation where the being has felt he has been running the body and making the decisions about your life. You can usually spot him because of his upsets at all the things that are going wrong with your life and your body. He has been going through the motions of operating the body, but he has not mastered the controls for the body and his actual role is that of a back seat driver who sees trouble but cannot take action to prevent it. Whenever you desire to do something new or risky, the negative emotion you feel is coming from this being.

The second situation exists when you and another being have been operating in tandem for a very long time. You have spent so many lifetimes together in this arrangement that you do not recognize you are separate beings. You have developed complementary skills to handle any situation and the relationship is so smooth that you are both unaware of the other and see no need to change until some session reveals a difference between you regarding the outcome of some action.

The beings who think they are you can have a wide range of capabilities and problems. Fortunately, we do not have to invent a new version of Talking to Spirits to handle each one. The same general approach works on all of them.

When you run into a being that says he is you, great care must be taken not to invalidate the being or his identity. The easiest way to begin is to ask how long has the being had this identity and was there some incident when it began.

If you approach this being in a caring way, the truth will emerge eventually and everyone involved will be able to take responsibility for their part in creating the situation. The bottom line is that all of these situations were the result of someone trying to "solve a problem".

I was working with a client who had a being who was running the left side of his body. The client was athletically oriented and participated in all sorts of sports even though he was hampered by a "weakness" in the left side of his body. The being attempting to control the left side of the body was an intellectual who preferred reading to all other activities.

The client was the stronger being and could force the other being to comply when he competed in events. The weaker being would fight back by making the left leg drag its foot and through other means of opposition.

The client no longer competes in athletic events and we handled the source of the resistance from the left side spirit. They had once been brothers who were very competitive and after dying in a long ago battle, they still competed.

When it became time to pick up a new body, neither would not let go once they took hold of the baby's body. They formed an uneasy alliance, but resisted each others efforts to control the body without acknowledging that they were separate beings.

This is not an unusual situation. We quite often discover a being attached to a body and thinking that he is the one rightful owner of the body. The confusion is easily sorted out once spiritual counseling is done.

Many of the beings you encounter
when talking to spirits
have forgotten that they were independent beings.

They may still be carrying old identities around
but they may consider these identities
part of your memories.

After all, until this moment in session,
you have been considering these memories
part of your own history.

It takes caring communication
to ease a spirit into shifting his considerations
and getting him to realize
he is no longer a Confederate soldier
but an immortal spirit who is a living thought.

When this shift in awareness occurs
you have the responsibility
to restore his free will
and prepare him for a new future.

SESSION EXAMPLES - MORE BEINGS YOU CANNOT HANDLE BY YOURSELF

1. An unhappy spirit driving away customers.
A client was reciting the problems he was having with new customers, so I asked him what he was doing that was bringing in so many unsatisfied customers.

He couldn't answer that but went on to say that the customers didn't want to pay what they had agreed to pay and they didn't have any money, etc., etc., and weren't reliable, etc.

He was really upset and resentful at the treatment he was getting from these customers and could not let go of the feeling.

When I asked him if he really cared about these customers, he grudgingly said they were very hard to deal with.

Then after many tries to get him to look at what he was actually doing that might have created these unpleasant customer relationships, I finally asked if he made any effort to find out more about them before doing business with them.

At this point, the client blurted out the following statement: "If that's the case, I might as well give up on being an Lawyer!"

This statement, after 15 successful years in his profession, did not sound like the generous and warm professional I knew. It sounded like an unhappy youngster stomping off to his bedroom after not getting his way.

It was so non sequitur that I asked if that was him or a spiritual being speaking, and he immediately spotted that it was an spirit.

The spirit, whose name was Derek, had actually been with him for a very long time and had failed as an attorney because he didn't communicate with his clients. His failure has so embittered him that he did not believe clients could be trusted and he was interfering with all of my client's customer relationships.

My client would establish a friendly relationship with a prospect and Derek would act to poison the relationship by inserting hostile flows into the conversation at every opportunity.

Once Derek was handled, my client became his usual warm self again and all traces of the resentful and hostile Derek had vanished.

2. A Spiritual Whipping Boy

The client has been on my lines for many years and we have always known there was a part of his case that was not being touched by anything we have run.

As we have continued to run spiritual counseling sessions things have been definitely opening up little by little. In this session he made an observation that in running things in session, "My stuff is always black."

When I asked if that was an implant, he originated that there has always been a spirit involved as long as we have been auditing and then he said, "He is me!"

He said he had this twin who he spun off to be the being who set the standards for behavior but they got very angry with each other.

After that the client punished the other "Me" by dumping all of the experiences he didn't want to remember on him. He made the other "me" a "whipping boy" by dumping all the bad memories on him and blanking out his own memories in those areas.

He realized in the session that uploading all of those painful and embarrassing memories to the other being was creating clusters of disturbed spirits on the other being.

By the end of the session the client was beginning to have all sorts of realizations about his life and the long term difficulties he had with counseling of all kinds. He is not finished yet.

He is still trying to grapple with the problems he created for his twin being and for himself by sequestering troubled beings around his "whipping boy" and blanking out his memories of what he had done.

This is not a unique situation. A being can create imaginative solutions for problems they do not wish to confront, but the problems do not go away until the being takes responsibility for what he has done and discovers why he did what he did.

When you take on the task of talking to the spirit in a caring way, you help him discover how he trapped himself with his efforts to avoid responsibility.

3. Loss of a Dear Friend or Family Member

If someone has departed this world, but an overpowering feeling of loss lingers on, this is probably because you and they did not achieve closure because of the manner of their death.

There are times when we lose a loved one and the grief subsides over time and we can put our attention toward rebuilding our life in their absence.

However, there are too many other times when waves of grief sweep over us unexpectedly for years afterwards and the feeling of loss is almost too much to bear.

Our research has shown that if you are still grieving for a lost loved one, that person has not been able to move on either and is still trying to reach you and achieve closure on some important matter. Fortunately, you can contact them if you wish, and finish your conversations using spiritual counseling from a friend.

I have been teaching people how to communicate with spirits for many years and talking to spirits is one of the most easily learned methods for relieving this kind of spiritual distress.

You may be able to handle the person in a solo session, but it will be faster and less painful if you let someone assist you in talking to a dear departed spirit.

4. A being who has cravings that you can't resist

This was one of my beings and until I got a session from my friend Kathy, I never knew why I had this particular craving.

I would be reading a book and give myself an hour to read it and by the time I get done with the book, it is three hours later and it was two in the morning.

197

Kathy helped me to locate the being who gave me this need to read until a book is done.

Her name was Evelyn. Evelyn had been alive during World War II and she loved to read. She had been a librarian, but during World War II the circumstances were such that she couldn't get anything to read. When she died, she was very frustrated that she had not been able to get anything to read.

She stumbled upon me in a library where I worked when I was in junior high school. I had a job where I put the books back on the shelves. She just attached herself to me because I could read very rapidly and was willing to read anything and everything.

I would be putting a book away and if it attracted her attention, she would get me to open the book and I would read it standing up until the librarian would come and find me reading in the book stacks and say, "David, why aren't you working?"

And, it was because Evelyn had me reading!

Now, in this case with Evelyn, she did not need a whole lot of handling because she realized how she was affecting my present time performance. She was up tone and she was having realizations that she really loves to read and she wasn't helping me by keeping me up so late at night.

This was how simple this session was because there was no digging around for any kind of real trauma about her death, or any justifications for anything that she had done. She felt better because she could now hang out with me and read books!

One of the things I took away from this session was that you don't have to plod, plod, plod through everything, if you just let the spirit talk.

They can have realizations one after another and then you are done. You just tell him that you love them and that they can stay if they want or they can go play in the ocean.

5. You Are Not Going To Handle Self-Deprecation By Yourself

It is an urge, often an automatic and irresistible urge, to present yourself as lower than others, or less than you should be, or even invisible—unworthy of being seen.

If you find it hard to accept recognition or praise, you may the effect of this urge.

This was a very recent surprise discovery. Self-deprecation is not a minor affliction! Handling this problem can open the door to some major changes in a person.

It is a hidden obstacle to life that does not seem to be a big deal, but the source of your excessive modesty and inner "unworthiness" is very hard to spot and even harder to remove.

This behavior is caused by beings who see controlling you as a perfectly reasonable thing to do.

In most cases, you have been under their control for so many lifetimes that it seems perfectly normal to avoid being praised and to belittle your accomplishments at every opportunity, even when you have done an outstanding job.

It is an urge, often an automatic and irresistible urge, to present yourself as lower than others, or less than you should be, or even invisible—unworthy of being seen. If you find it hard to accept recognition or praise, you may the effect of this urge.

I have helped two clients to find and handle the beings that cause this behavior and they have had wins far greater than I would have ever expected.

If you do not feel comfortable about being praised or feel that you really aren't able to do anything special, you should give me a call and see if you are being controlled in this insidious way. You will not regret throwing off the control of these beings.

Self-deprecation is caused by
beings who see controlling you
as a perfectly reasonable thing to do.

In most cases,
you have been under their control
for so many lifetimes
that it seems perfectly normal
to avoid being praised
and to belittle your accomplishments
at every opportunity,
even when you have done an outstanding job.

A CHECKLIST TO SEE IF YOU ARE BEING CONTROLLED BY SPIRITS YOU CANNOT HANDLE BY YOURSELF

This list describes some indications that you may have some unhandled or unacknowledged spirits who are controlling your actions and behavior.

There are many more, but this should give you a good start in detecting these spirits.

1. Disclaimer
Be aware that these spirits are those who are in control of your life and actions and are causing results that you are not able to monitor or correct. You need to contact a professional Spiritual Counselor trained in Spiritual Rescue Technology processing to handle these beings.

This too, is a "Hot" list and is not for casual reading.

If you get a significant reaction to this list, DO NOT keep reading to see if you can get more reactions. When you read this list and get a reaction of any kind, you have triggered a past experience of a being who cannot be handled without professional help.

Note down what part of the checklist produced a reaction and what the reaction was in as much detail as possible. Do not do any other action until you contact a professional spiritual counselor trained in SRT counseling.

2. Follow this procedure to get best results.
This list should be run as follows: Starting anywhere on the list, read down the list and take up the very first example that indicates to you.

See if you can locate the spirit that is reacting to the list and note down what you can perceive for the spiritual counselor who will help you handle this being.

Do not be surprised if you cannot locate or identify the spirit who is reacting as these spirits are very difficult to handle even with professional help.

Note down what part of the checklist produced a reaction and what the reaction was in as much detail as possible. This way, the spiritual counselor will be able to duplicate your action and locate the being who is to be handled.

Do not look for another reaction after finding the first one.

You can look further after this first set of beings is handled by a spiritual counselor.

THE CHECKLIST OF BEHAVIORS

1. Inappropriate Emotional Reactions

A. You have occasional thoughts of committing suicide.

B. You have disgusting thoughts that you repress and you are unable to shake them off permanently.

C. There are things you have done in this lifetime that are so gross that you have never been able to share them with ANYBODY, even your most trusted friends. You have never figured out how you could have been so stupid or debased to have done what you did. (You had help)

D. Insistence on being right. (Remember that most of these spirits are trying to protect you.)

E. A fixed or stuck mood level that does not resolve when addressed.

F. Finding yourself asserting your spiritual superiority.

G. A Messiah Complex. You are out to save the world because only you have the answers to civilization's problems.

H. Periods when you have extremely destructive thoughts about someone or something and you toy with various ways to kill them or utterly destroy them.

I. You do not feel comfortable about being praised

2. Distractions

A. Doing and saying crazy things and then wonder where in the world that came from.

3. Compulsions

A. You find yourself drawn to certain people with an unbreakable sense of attraction. This is far more than simple admiration, it is a real compulsion, and you seem powerless to resist it.

B. You desire a substance and the desire is irresistible when you let down your guard. The substance could be coffee, chocolate, booze, cigarettes, and other drugs of every sort. The possibilities are endless but the manifestation is the same. You do not consider it an addiction but your attraction gets justified and you do it for years regardless of the effect on your health.

C. Your sexual urges cause you to desire and do antisocial acts, no matter how hard you try to resist it.

D. Finding yourself doing crazy things and wondering why you did them.

E. Decorating your body with extensive tattoos or inserted pieces of metal or bone.

F. You exhibit religious zeal or mania. You seek to convert people to whatever practice or philosophy you currently are following. You cannot leave them to their own political beliefs.

4. Aversions

A. Fear of certain types and races of people when there is no prior contact with them.

B. Hatred of certain types and races of people when there is no prior contact with them.

C. Certainty that women and certain races of people are inferior.

5. Inexplicable Events, Trends, Or Behavior

A. You are a top performer in your group or your job and yet people do not seem to appreciate you or acknowledge you. You get the feeling that everyone is out to get you and your job experiences and life experiences bear this out. You feel like you are operating under a curse.

B. You keep committing harmful acts on yourself and on others.

C. You speak and act in an exaggerated manner as though you are playing a part.

D. You refer to yourself in the third person.

E. You may have difficulty knowing who you really are. You may may have a sense that you are parked somewhere watching all of this go on.

F. You make less of your accomplishments at every opportunity.

6. Messages/Warnings

A. Discovering a behavior that indicates spiritual interference in your life and SUDDENLY feeling it is not important and should be ignored. (Something important has been made unimportant.)

B. Seeing futures as random thoughts or dreams that you would NOT like to experience. spirits can and will create futures that oppose what you would create for yourself. Going into agreement with their projected images is a sure way to bring about undesirable futures.

C. You get any of the following reactions on reading this list, either immediately or afterwards:

1. This information is dangerous and must be suppressed
2. I can use this to secure a competitive advantage in selling my services or product
3. With this data, I can control….
4. This group must not be allowed to…use this recklessly…benefit from this knowledge…post this information elsewhere…
5. Dreaming of scenarios involving "misuse" of this data
6. Fear of having this data widely understood and used

Conclusion

This checklist can be of help in spotting beings who are controlling you and are trying to stay out of sight, but it is not going to replace the services of a trained spiritual Counselor who has years of experience handling beings like this.

If you feel that your solo sessions are not going well and that Talking To Spirits is a crock of nonsense, you will feel like a new person when your counselor locates and handles the being who is dragging your morale down.

Any unhappy being can lower your confidence and make you feel gloomy about your future, but a being who is capable of controlling you is a real threat to your future and to your life if you do not get him help and bring him to present time where he can start a new life free of the compulsions of his past.

Remember, any being who is doing destructive actions is almost certainly acting from compulsions laid down many lifetimes ago. He is still fighting battles and monsters that have not existed for millennia and he will not be able to stop until he is brought safely into present time.

PHENOMENA TO EXPECT IN SPIRITUAL COUNSELING SESSIONS DONE TALKING TO SPIRITS STYLE

Spiritual counseling sessions done Talking To Spirits style creates a distinct set of phenomena that are not evident in other spiritual counseling practices. These phenomena do not appear in all sessions, but when they do appear, some of them can distract the unwary or inexperienced spiritual counselor because of their impact on the practitioner and his body.

When you are in good caring communication with spirits, all of the usual barriers are down. You are not parked safely behind a barrier of bored skepticism or trembling with fear or anxiety. If you are properly prepared, you are in present time and quite willing to share space with the beings you are talking to.

In a properly done Talking to Spirits session, you are sharing the thoughts and intentions of the beings you are talking to. As they describe what has happened to them, you are there and you can usually see what they were seeing at the time.

1. Instant Merging of Consciousness
You will even find that you may get a full history of the individual as a concentrated burst of information when you first encounter him. This can be a bit disconcerting at first, because you suddenly have his whole life available to you with his motivations and secret dreams laid bare in the first instants of encountering him.

It does not seem to be a two way merge, but the other person seems to become more comfortable with you when this occurs.

You still have to get the spirit to identify the incident that is holding his attention and controlling his thoughts, but you will know what you are looking for as you already know what the incident is and what he did to trigger the incident.

What is generally not visible is his justification for doing what he did to begin the long dwindling spiral over many lifetimes and that is because he does not know why he did it. In the session, you will help him discover why he did the fateful action that caused all of the other things to happen.

2. Unconsciousness
There are some spirits who are enveloped in so much unconsciousness that this can be the first sign that a spiritual being is present. The counselor asks if there is an spirit involved and the client says, "No" or "Yes" and then yawns. When this occurs, the counselor can also be hit with the same unconsciousness as he attempts to run the counseling process.

Both client and counselor will find themselves yawning uncontrollably while running the session, but if they continue without getting distracted by the occasional jaw breaking yawns, they will handle the spirit and all will end well.

Some may think this is an example of "being unprofessional", meaning that the counselor is allowing himself to experience the feelings and unconsciousness of the spiritual beings. These people do not realize that successful communication with spiritual beings REQUIRES that the counselor be willing to BE the spirit and to experience what the spirit is feeling.

Attempting to run a spiritual counseling session while fixed in an "unfeeling, can't be effect of anything that happens" mood will not give any being a sense that they are being heard and understood.

Those who suffered through counseling sessions delivered by people trained to be unfeeling robots will remember the frustration of realizing that your counselor did not understand what you had just said.

3. Grief
Grief in spiritual counseling Talking to Spirits style can be as intense as in any other spiritual counseling system but clients will notice that they can switch from deep grief with heavy sobs and tears spurting from their eyes to a quietly objective recounting of how this relates to their current life and then back into incoherent sobs again.

This phenomenon springs from the fact that the grief is NOT the clients grief. He is misowning the grief of the being he is communicating with and he can experience the grief even though the grief is not his. All he has to do is to withdraw from the communication a little bit and the grief will subside.

If the counselor wants to free the being from the incident and its resulting emotional burden, the counselor has to duplicate the incident and its effects to know when it is completely handled.

4. Transfer of Spiritual Beings from Client to Counselor and Back

Occasionally in session, the counselor will notice that a large mass has settled over his face or other part of his body. This can occur when a cluster feels that the counselor provides an opportunity that the client does not provide. This can also occur if a counselor and the spirits being handled have an affinity for each other.

If any of you are delivering a spiritual counseling session and you feel the presence of additional spirits or clusters, just acknowledge their presence and continue the session by delivering your communication to wherever they are now located.

Occasionally I have relieved a client of a mass or a cluster that the client could not handle or communicate with and ended the session with the agreement that I would complete the handling off line.

In a few sessions, I have had spirits jump from the client to me during the session, possibly out of curiosity, and I would discuss this with the client and would continue the session with the spirits in my space rather than in the client's space.

The client could perceive where the spirits had moved to and would direct his attention appropriately. In some cases, the spirit would return to the client where he would remain to work with the client as part of his spiritual partner team.

5. Pulling In Spirits From Other People And Distant Places
If someone has attention on someone else, it is possible for that person to bring spirits from that someone else and communicate with them as easily as if the spirit is one of their own.

These spirits can be on someone who currently has a body, or from a recently deceased relative or friend. This can be done in a solo session, but it is easier if you are working with a spiritual counselor.

6. Distinct Messages from Spirits
You will be in session and you get a clear message that the client or an spirit is hiding something important, or you suddenly get an explanation for something that the client is trying to explain. These messages can come from your spirits or from spirits associated with the client. Once you learn to trust these messages, counseling becomes a lot easier.

7. Experiencing an incident, permeating all of it and achieving total duplication
This is similar to experiencing an individual's entire life in one burst of data, and it makes it easy to help a being recover his memories of the incident.

The way I experience this phenomena is that I ask for the incident, and I get the incident as a single concept, not as a narrative produced by the being.

For example, I ask "Is there an incident you have attention on?" and I see a spaceship disintegrating with debris jetting out of it and I know a mistake was made. After that, it is an easy matter to find out more.

8. Encountering Gods And Demons From Every Nation's Legends

There are beings who are, quite frankly, overwhelming if you are not a professional counselor. You will encounter Gods and Demons from every nation's legends and you will find that they are real and did things that are impossible to comprehend.

They have lost most of their powers over millennia of self-destructive behavior, but they have been responsible for some of the worst chapters in our planetary history.

They are not to be treated lightly because they are some of the most powerful beings ever to grace this planet. They have fallen to a lower state, like all of us, but they can be rehabilitated so they can contribute to the future like all of the other beings we are able to contact.

This caring handling can also be used when a beings says he is GOD or LUCIFER. If you ask in a caring way, "What problem does being GOD solve?", you will get some surprising answers and will help the being in ways you never expected.

Here are some examples:

8.1. A Recent Conversation with Marduk

Marduk is one of the more fascinating beings we have encountered in recent months.

Although he presented himself as a demon at first, dedicated to ruining a client's life, when I was finally able to engage him in conversation, Marduk turned out to be one of the many Annunaki gods who show up in Sumerian mythology.

At the height of his power, he was a force to be reckoned with but over millennia he became more and more degraded until he was fixed in a state where he hated everything, including himself.

His story was remarkably similar to other beings who consider they are the epitome of evil. Long before he became a minor deity in the Babylonian legends, he had originally been a wild and creative being whose creations offended and scared more conservative beings.

These conservative beings arranged to trap him and convinced him he was guilty of antisocial acts and that he could never be redeemed unless he would become an instrument of punishment against "sinners".

In his various incarnations, he became a powerful force for dealing out punishment and even participated in the tortures perpetrated on criminals and sinners during the Inquisition. He provided some interesting insights why members of the Holy Orders indulged in the depths of depravity and torture. His feeling was that it allowed them to release their inner demons and would leave them purified

He seemed to have surfaced again in the era of the Marquis de Sade, where his degradation was almost complete and he was no longer able to maintain his own body.

I was able to take him back to when he was a purely spiritual being and was overwhelmed by a group of beings he wanted to join. He wanted their admiration for his creativity and they withheld their admiration and mocked him until he went into agreement with them and admired their creations instead of his own.

Once he compromised his personal integrity, they were able to overwhelm him and make him degrade himself in order to win their praise.

By getting his justifications for agreeing to that first degradation, I was able to get him to the point where he wanted to leave my client alone and go off to a quiet place off planet where he could think about things.

8.2. Alien Beings of All Kinds

If you run enough spiritual counseling sessions, you will run into alien beings who were lizard people or Reptilians and Annunaki and who played major parts in creating and destroying civilizations here on Earth and elsewhere.

We spirits were all Annunakis and Reptilian Gods at one point. Most of us pretend that we can't remember any of that stuff and we shudder when someone brings it up again. Just use caring communication in your solo sessions and a lot of your past history will heave into view.

You will also encounter alien beings who used to have insect-like bodies and fish bodies as well as alien beings who used to operate mechanical bodies. The handling is the same, no matter what or who they were. We free them from the incidents they are still stuck in and bring them to present time and restore their free will.

We are now focused on helping them regain some of their original abilities so they can contribute to the future course of events on Earth.

This not an exhaustive set of session phenomena, but this should prepare you when you encounter some sort of anomaly in session.

FINAL REMARKS

1. Life On A Haunted Planet
What are the upsides to living on a planet populated with immortal beings?

There are an almost infinite number of talented beings to observe and learn from. Most of them do not have bodies.

Not all beings choose to be human lifetime after lifetime. Some choose to be disembodied spirits and play a role of advising and helping those who are running bodies and are in need of advice.

My current rough estimate is that there are a trillion disembodied spirits for every spirit running a body.

Disembodied spirits are distributed everywhere on Earth, but seem to be concentrated around areas of conflict or where much loss of life has occurred. Each of us who have bodies are accompanied by an entourage of spiritual beings in various states of awareness.

Many of these spirits are unconscious or sleeping and only become active when they are activated by present time incidents that resonate with them.

Some disembodied spirits are fully aware and are heavily involved in the lives of living organisms either as mentors, monitors, spirit guides, or even vengeful tormentors.

From what we have seen in sessions, the average person has from 5 to 25 spirits who help the person play the role he has chosen in life. You might say that these are teammates who put on the show that is you in real life.

Unfortunately, for most people, these spirits are not organized into a team. They are more likely to be a disorganized mob where each tries to take control when the opportunity arises.

You have beings who are into eating, others are into sex, others who are into reading fiction, others who are religious... the list goes on and on. Most of the time these beings merely influence you, but occasionally they will take control if they feel an emergency has occurred.

If you have ever been goaded beyond your limits, you can probably remember changing from your usual timid self into someone strong and fearless who put an immediate stop to your punishment and walked out and created a new future. It will seem as if you changed into a sort of a super being who would take no more insults and was able to walk out of the situation and create a new life starting immediately.

That super self had been lurking in the background all along and only appeared when you were pushed too far and humiliated to the point where you lost control of yourself. Typically, the super being will continue to run things until the danger is past and then you will slump back into your old timid habits.

This book provides the tools which enable you to heal your troubled beings and to enhance your helpful beings so that they can work as a well-coordinated team.

Once you start communicating with your helpful beings and get them to work as a team, you will find that you are able to handle life with ease and accomplish more than ever before. The power of aligned intentions has to be seem to be believed. You will experience complete certainty perhaps for the first time in your life and formerly difficult activities will become easy and pleasurable.

You can view the hordes of disembodied spirits as a threat and be suitably overwhelmed, or you can view these spirits as a resource to be helped and trained for specific duties and look forward to a life of ease and great accomplishments.

If you search diligently, you may find Archimedes, Voltaire, Genghis Khan, Alexander the Great, Tesla, and many others to draw upon for inspiration and advice. Continuing Talking to Spirit sessions will provide the tools for you to acquire knowledge from the beings who helped create the world as it exists today.

2. Suppose owning bodies for life might be a complete falsehood

Suppose that all that we have been told about beings and bodies is conjecture?

The whole idea of history is that we form tribes and beget children to carry on our tribal traditions and customs and to preserve a place on the earth for our children and their children after them.

The usual sequence of events that has been understood is that we pick up the body at birth and we stick with it until the body dies and then we go pick up another body or hang out as a disembodied spirit for a very long time.

This simplistic explanation does not begin to explain the different tales we get from many spirits.

For example, in wartime some soldiers are killed and instead of flying home to see how the family is doing, they pick up an unconscious soldier body and reanimate it in an effort to get back into action without delay.

There are other beings who do not want to animate a baby body and go through the diapers and school phase before they can get busy again. They will hang around hospitals and places where people are injured in the hopes of finding a new body whose animating spirit is absent or unconscious. When they find a suitably unconscious body, they take over the motor controls and pretend to be the previous owner.

These enterprising beings are called walk-ins because they pick up a body when the original spirit is no longer capable of controlling it.

This can occur when a person is extremely ill, or unconscious from drugs or poisons, or has received a great shock or injury.

I am a walk-in and I know several other walk-ins. I was chatting with a client I have known for thirty years and he reminded me that I had audited him about his being a walk-in many years ago.

We started wondering how many walk-ins exist who do not know they are walk-ins because they picked up their bodies when the body was very young. At this point, I started wondering how many people came home from a hospital after surgery with a new attitude on life and never realized that they were under the control of a new set of spiritual beings.

Suddenly, we had this joint realization that the "normal view" of people owning bodies for life might be a complete falsehood. Suppose the whole matter of spirits animating bodies was more like a giant Airbnb** arrangement, where spirits cruised the planet and picked up bodies for short term enjoyment and education.

**Airbnb is a peer-to-peer online marketplace and homestay network that enables people to list or rent short-term lodging in residential properties, with the cost of such accommodation set by the property owner. (Wikipedia)

As this realization hit us, we both broke into peals of laughter and felt a similar reaction going on with the beings in our space. What we formerly saw as living bodies that we owned suddenly became more like timeshare properties!

I have not had time to address all of the ramifications of this realization, but there definitely is a broadening of the viewpoint I have on my "life".

This also explained why I am no fan of astral travel or true exteriorization (out of body activity). I do not want to leave my body unattended for any length of time. If I could take this body over when the original occupant was out of commission, then leaving this body unattended might result in my being occupied by someone else in my absence.

As for perceiving remote locations, I can do that quite well by sending spiritual partners to take a look and send back images. As we end sessions and send beings off to remote locations, we often get a glimpse of the destination as the being homes in on that location.

3. Spiritual Beings Constantly Affect Your Behavior, Health, And Personality.

If a person does not get this, he or she will think Talking to Spirits is wonderful but will keep looking for other solutions to handle the really "difficult" problems like migraines, PMS, cheating husbands, illnesses, hangnails, etc., etc.

Now you can either decide to be the effect of all these spiritual beings, or you can decide to manage them for your benefit.

Talking to Spirits provides all of the tools you will need to help your spirits contribute to your welfare or to set them free to create independent lives of their own.

The spirits who surround you can be a resource or a nightmare depending on how you treat them.

If you foolishly try to get rid of the spiritual beings who surround you, you might end up like others who have tried this, sick and miserable due to the counter intentions of unhappy spiritual beings. These beings do not like being scraped off.

Talking to Spirits will give you the tools you need to create a better existence for you and for your spiritual companions.

When you are ready to dig further into the underlying technology behind Talking To Spirits, you are invited to investigate the Appendix, which describes Spiritual Rescue Technology and provides links to the books and websites containing all that has been written about this technology.

May you be inspired to do your own research into our spiritual companions and their affect on our past and future existence.

David St Lawrence

AKASHIC RECORDS OF THE PAST, PRESENT, AND FUTURE

When you can read the Akashic Records, you can observe the past, present, and future activities of any spirit anywhere.

Understanding This Book Will Enable You To Read Akashic Records
Our Spiritual Rescue Technology research reveals that we can easily talk to any spirit and locate important events that occurred in his past and what he intends to create in the future.

All it takes is an ability to operate in Present Time, use Caring Communication, and know how to use Reaching and Withdrawing to connect with any being or situation.

Once you can reach and withdraw from a being or a situation, you can actually duplicate what the being is doing and what his intentions are. Since all beings are living thoughts, you are able to duplicate what this being has thought and done for his entire existence. This means that you are reading his Akashic Records.

> *In theosophy and anthroposophy, the Akashic records are a compendium of all human events, thoughts, words, emotions, and intent ever to have occurred in the past, present, or future. They are believed by theosophists to be encoded in a non-physical plane of existence known as the etheric plane.*

To put this in simple terms, the Akashic Records are the collection of everyone's time track, everywhere. All thoughts, intentions, actions from the past, present, and future.

Another way of looking at these records is realizing they are a multichannel recording of all beings in this universe and they extend into the future as far as the beings are willing to create them. Our futures unroll before us as we postulate them or intend them. Thus a skilled reader of thoughts can see how much future a person or group is creating.

The future will happen to the extent that there is agreement among the people who will be living that future.

This also shows what is happening to the being who is stuck in a past moment. He is not creating a future and may be holding others back from doing so. If you are surrounded by beings stuck in the past, it can hinder you from achieving your goals.

The Akashic Records Are Being Created Continuously
Now that we have discovered that we can read the record of any being's existence and his projected future, what does this mean for the future of our research? It could mean that we now have a glimpse of the connectedness that exists between spirits and an overall view of patterns of life force that will allow us to predict futures for individuals, groups and civilizations and to modify those futures in ways we did not suspect before this moment.

To repeat my earlier observation, the Akashic Records are the collection of everyone's time track, everywhere. All thoughts, intentions, actions from the past, present, and future are recorded in the spiritual universe and are accessible to those who can read thoughts. These recordings include moments of joy and moments of incredible overwhelm and terror.

What sets those of us who understand Spiritual Rescue Technology apart from the scholars and philosophers of the past is that we know that those of us who are running bodies are composite beings. The Akashic Records we access are multi-being recordings. We can access the records of every one of the beings who consider they are part of our personality.

Since we are immortal and our spiritual companions are immortal, there is an enormous amount of data at our disposal when we choose to look. Even our everyday memories are colored and influenced by the beings who are part of our composite personality.

Those of us who have been able to bring most of our spiritual companions up to present time, can experience life and it's surprises with an amazing amount of equanimity. Any one who has not talked to their spirits and handled the incidents that can cripple them emotionally will encounter rude surprises when life is upsetting, because present day upset can trigger old incidents that caused death and destruction for the beings who accompany you.

Which brings us to the most important part of the Akashic Records. From what we are able to observe, the records are being continually created with emotions, intentions, regrets, and accomplishments. The being who is operating in present time, is laying down a recording that conforms to what is actually happening as time passes.

The being who is still stuck in a horrific incident that overwhelmed him a long time ago, is recording that incident over and over again as a continuous creation. As far as that being is concerned, he is still experiencing the explosion, or execution by firing squad that ended his life.

It is the experience of being overwhelmed that makes time seem to stop for the being. The passage through time and space continues but he is continually creating that moment over and over again. If he is able to experience what is happening today, it seems as if it is a dream. Reality is the bullets from the firing squad which are still ripping through him.

You, who are running a body and struggling to operate in present time, have a certain number of beings who are still stuck in some past incident. If something in your current environment resembles a part of their earlier, fatal incident, they will react as if the incident was occurring again.

Visiting historical sites, or prisons, even hospitals can set off some of your spiritual companions. With a little training in Spiritual Rescue Technology, you will be able to tell when a spirit has been triggered by a present day event and you will be able to calm him down by acknowledging his distress. When you have time, you can visit the part of his Akashic Records that have been activated and help him sort it out so it does not bother him any more.

I mentioned earlier that the Akashic Records seem to have recordings of future events. This phenomena has been reported by earlier researchers and there are psychics who offer readings of a person's Akashic Records including records of future events.

Our observations indicate that the future is created by the intentions and postulates of these who will be experiencing it. A person can create a future through intentions that extends for months and even years. Other people can only envision what they will be doing tomorrow or later today if they are in bad shape. I have run a few experiments with family and staff members to verify that coordinated intentions produce future events.

Now that we have a more complete view of Akashic Records, we can make better observations of the future a person and his spiritual companions are projecting. Taking the intentions and purposes of the entire group into account will make it easier to produce the future the person wants. A future is the joint creation of the person running the body and all of his awake and aware spiritual companions. If the person learns to get agreement with his desires, he will experience the desired future. If the person is being opposed by his spiritual companions, he will be continually frustrated at his failure to achieve his goals.

Our research also indicates that the Akashic Records are mutable, that is to say they can be changed or perhaps overlaid by new data. We observe that a being is kept in a fixed state or a fixed emotion by some past event, but when we investigate the event with caring communication and run a simple Spiritual Rescue Technology process, the being is freed from overwhelm of the incident and regains his free will and emotional stability.

The same occurs when we look at a projected future, or the absence of an ability to create a future. Running a Spiritual Rescue Technology process on the situation enables the creation of a desired future where this was not possible before.

How Do We Create The Akashic Records?
The Akashic Records contains every thought, emotion, intention, and effort of every being's existence.

When you begin to access someone's Akashic Records, the immensity of the person's existence becomes very real to you. You see the circumstances of his birth and his conception, and if you look further you will see his earlier lifetimes in exact detail as far as he is interested in looking.

The records vary in intensity, depending on his level of life force and emotion at the time in question.

A being who spent most of his lifetime in quiet meditation would probably leave a quiet record of peaceful thoughts, where a tormented soul might leave a record filled with incidents of screaming rage and incessant pain.

Almost anyone who can receive thoughts can detect Akashic Records containing lots of emotion. When these people are around friends who are not doing well, they are almost compelled to ask, "Is everything all right? Are you OK?"

Some spiritual counselors can read a client's Akashic Records like a book. More expert counselors can tell whether the Akashic Record belongs to the person or one of the spirits who accompany the person through life. A non-judgmental discussion of the emotionally charged incident will usually cause a release of attention and the person no longer will have stuck attention on the incident.

A Spiritual Rescue Technology counselor is able to engage the troubled spirit in discussion about the incident he is fixated on and to resolve any issues and confusions that has trapped his attention on that moment in time. Once the spirit is able to take his attention off the incident that overwhelmed him, his free will returns and he is able to operate fully in present time.

The Spiritual Rescue Technology counselor is able to see when the being is freed from the incident because the being is no longer continually creating that incident.

When an SRT counselor looks at a client who is not operating fully in present time, he sees that the client and some of his beings have attention on some incident that is not part of the current present time environment. Simply asking what the person's attention is stuck on will often bring the incident into view where it can be handled in session.

The spiritual universe becomes much more comprehensible when you consider it to be composed of Akashic Records, all being continually created by the beings in the spiritual universe. It offers the promise that any action anywhere can be recovered and analyzed if the seeker of information can raise their awareness sufficiently.

Using The Akashic Records To Recover Data
Remember that the Akashic Records are the collection of everyone's time track, everywhere. All thoughts, intentions, actions from the past, present, and future are recorded in the spiritual universe and are accessible to those who can read thoughts.

Every moment of every recording can be taken as the subjective truth of what happened, since the recording is what the observer EXPERIENCES at that particular moment.

If the person was under a hypnotic spell, or a pain drug hypnosis implant, or heavily drugged, his record of the experience may be different than the actual experience.

If there were observers of the experience, there will be Akashic Records of their observations and since almost all persons on this planet are accompanied by a crowd of spirits, there is almost always multiple records of every moment in time. Thus the totality of the Akashic Records of any incident can be examined to find the truth of what happened and how it was caused.

Once the truth of an incident is known, all confusion is blown and the incident is merely a memory, not a problem to be solved. The person sees their responsibility in causing the incident they have been fixated on and they no longer create it in an effort to understand what happened.

If we choose to investigate how the person or being got into the situation he is suffering from, we only need to go earlier and see what the person or being did or failed to do that caused the episode to happen.

If that does not unstick him from trying to understand what happened, we ask the person or being how he justified doing or failing to do what he did to cause the incident that changed his life forever.

We have to persist in asking for the justification for triggering the life changing event until the person or being breaks into laughter. He will realize that he made a life destroying decision because he couldn't think of anything else to do.

His justification usually falls along the line of, "It seemed like a good idea at the time!" or "I was desperate and couldn't think of anything else I could do!"

Spiritual Counseling Using The Akashic Records

A person can be stuck in an poor emotional state because of a past event from childhood or from many lifetimes ago. Introducing the concept of the Akashic Records and the possibility of seeking answers from these records can give the client a framework to understand the images and thoughts he will encounter in session.

It also provides a framework to introduce the client to the idea he is immortal and has lived many lifetimes.

A client new to counseling can be quite overwhelmed when he pulls up an incident in response to what seems like a simple question. If he is prepared by introducing him to the concept that there are Akashic Records and they have been observed and documented for hundreds of years, he may even look forward to sighting some evidence of these records.

You should be aware that a person or being can forget or suppress any memory of his Akashic Records, especially if they were very painful. Since, in most cases, the person's spiritual companions will have a record of the painful incident, if you are a trained spiritual counselor you will be able to see the incident even if the person can't.

This is why, when you ask a client for a particular incident that you are aware of, he may not recall it at first, but with gentle questioning he will be able to pull up the incident and how it occurred. It was so terrible or shameful that he shut it out of his memory but with your gentle assistance it will emerge so he can deal with it.

Here are some examples of how to use the Akashic Records to help others:

The Stolen Baby:
I was helping a new client to address a complete hatred of his entire family. He was in his late 40s and had always hated his mother and father and didn't know why.

I asked him to go back to the first moment he realized he hated his family and he said, "I am sitting on the floor in my diaper looking at a rat under my bed!"

I had him go earlier to his birth and the rest of the story popped into view.

He was a handsome and healthy baby and a nurse has stolen him and raised him as her own because she could not have babies. His father and mother were wealthy and the father was a doctor and the birth took place in a hospital in Boston.

The client could hardly believe when he was seeing, but the rat under his bed made a huge impression on him. He followed up on the matter and found that his mother did not have a birth certificate for him.

A Client Was Never Treated Like The Rest Of The family:
A client had always tried to excel for her father and mother, but never seemed to get the recognition she deserved. Other siblings always got praised for their efforts, but she got the barest acknowledgment even though she was the most successful of all of the children.

She was the youngest child. There were several other siblings and she was the youngest by 6 years.

I had her look earlier to see what had happened and she said her mother had wanted to abort her as she did not want more children.

I asked this client why she chose these parents and she brightened up and said, "Mother was beautiful and my father was very intelligent and they were well off! "

When I asked how her mother got pregnant, the client realized that she had made that happen. She had carefully chosen her parents, but had never gotten their agreement to her appearance as their child. She can do that now if she chooses.

Clients Who Feel They Are Cursed:

I often run into clients who feel they are cursed, and lo and behold, they have managed to become cursed by actions they did in earlier life times. With an understanding of the Akashic Records, these actions can be located.

This is the way it works. When people are killed unfairly, or through treachery, or in a truly despicable way, they hold a grudge. People who have been tortured to death will haunt the perpetrators forever, no matter what peaceful career the perpetrator has taken up in future lives.

People killed in battle may not expect to be killed, but that is one of the things that happens in wars. If a unit is betrayed by their leaders, the dead often want to get even and they will haunt whoever betrayed them.

When people die in battle, they do not expect to see their bodies be mutilated and otherwise violated after death. Those who order this mutilation are often haunted by the spirits of the dead, who may follow them for many lifetimes counter-intending anything the person does.

The cursed clients may now be living blameless lives, but the ungrateful dead still wish them harm. The more people they have harmed, the greater the effect of being haunted.

Lifting the curse requires the cursed person to revisit the atrocities he has caused and to take responsibility for causing the atrocity or failing to stop the atrocity.

So-called innocent bystanders are often haunted by victims of an atrocity because they bystanders did nothing to prevent it from happening. Lifting a curse requires recognizing that you are cursed and locating what you have done to become cursed.

Managing The Future Using The Akashic Records

We have already mentioned that Akashic Records extend into the future and can be accessed by those who are sufficiently trained. This opens the door to understanding how to manage the future to accomplish what you want.

These Records are created by the actions and intentions of spiritual beings. Those of you who have learned how to talk to spirits have been accessing these records for some time. You have probably noticed that the recording intensity does not depend on when the recording was made, but on the emotion accompanying the event.

In other words, an image from the Akashic Records seems to be clearer and more intense if more life force was expended at that moment.

You can verify for yourself how the clarity of an Akashic Record varies with the emotion and life force involved in making the record

During spiritual counseling sessions I have seen images from exploding spaceships that were bright and crisp even though the images were not mine. I saw an image from the First World War that was completely three dimensional, but that was one of my recordings.

On the other hand, a great many of the images I see in session are quite faint and the thoughts that I perceive range from almost silent to impossible to ignore.

If the clarity of an Akashic Record is dependent on the life force we put into creating it, this may explain why Akashic Records of the future are so faint. They are tentatively created.

From my personal experiences when exploring the future, the clearest images occurred when my necessity level was raised out of great need.

As a reasonable alternative to resorting to desperate measures, I found that we can see future occurrences by locating something we know is going to happen, and after meditating to a calm state, seeking to perceive HOW is was going to happen. Doing this with people who are going to be involved in the result seems to produce the best results.

Here are two examples:

Buying A Car: My wife and I absolutely needed to buy an automobile, and we knew we would drive it home after we purchased it. We looked at the streets we might be driving home on and one was the obvious choice. We set out down that street toward the area of the city where autos were sold looking for a car. We found the exact car we wanted at the first car lot we came to. There was this Crown Victoria sitting there waiting for us and we drove it for several years.

Moving A Dianetic Center: Our Dianetics Center was located in an area of Los Angeles which was becoming unsafe, so we decided to move. I held a meeting of the staff and I discussed what we were looking for in our new location and got their agreement. Then I asked them to look at this future event and see what truck would be used to move us and what street it would take to our new location.

As soon as we began looking at the future event, we could see a particular truck parked at the front door and the staff identified who owned it. We were also able to track the truck as it drove away to the new site. We got in our cars after the meeting and drove to where the truck image vanished.

There was space for rent in a safe area over a coffee shop. I rented the new space and I called the owner of the truck and he agreed to move us.

The move was successful, but the truck took an unexpected detour which made us realize that the future is the result of all of the intentions of the people creating it. The truck driver decided to drive his truck down a small flight of stairs instead of backing it out to the parking lot he had come from.

What this means is that the future is constantly mutable. If you can envision a future occurrence and actually see how people are located and dressed, you may find that when the magic moment arrives that the people are standing in different places than you envisioned and some are wearing different clothes.

Increasing Your Understanding of the Spirit World
Knowing that there are related recordings of every action by every spirit opens the door to a different understanding of the connectedness of all spiritual beings.

If a person knows where to look to connect with a particular spirit's Akashic Recording, he should be able to expand his view to see what other spirits were doing at that same moment.

Just being aware that there is an Akashic Record for every existing being brings up the possibility that one could connect with any spirit and initiate caring communication with that spirit if the spirit agreed to be communicated with.

Since spirits are immortal, one should be able to connect with Aristotle, or Archimedes, or Saint Thomas Aquinas for that matter, and see what they might be willing to share.

The possibilities, and the challenges, are endless.

ACKNOWLEDGEMENTS

This book could not have been written without the help of the many people who supported me and gave me advice while I was building a spiritual counseling practice and documenting my discoveries of the spiritual realm.

First and foremost is the support I have received from my wife Gretchen during my long transition from a Scientology Mission Holder to corporate executive and then to full time spiritual counselor while developing Spiritual Rescue Technology.

I would not have been able to write this book without the support of long time friends like David Marlow, Scott Weible, Herbert Druker, Jim Spaetti, Kathy Elliott, Ron Bible, Sheila Lanier, Brett Falicon, and many others who helped me unravel the mysteries of the spirit world while we were working with their spiritual companions.

This book is the result of thoughtful review and editing by Nolan Cage, my remarkable proofreader, and much advice and many suggestions from Shirley Bleau, Alka Chopra Madan, Jack Airey, Al Leggett, Denetra Rodriguez, Petra Held, Stephen Sarocky, and Lars Wefringhaus.

Many of the foregoing also contributed by participating in my weekly webinar sessions where we advanced the state of our spiritual knowledge by exchanging information we obtained from our spiritual partners. It became evident over this last year that our spiritual partners were playing a more significant role in our lives as time passed.

This may not be the first book where spirits are acknowledged for their contribution, but it surely will not be the last. As I indicated in the preface to this book, the data contained here is from conversations with spirits in and out of session.

235

The marvelous cover is the work of Diane Dutra who managed to convey the feeling of what talking to spirits can do. The background graphic is called Man's Journey of the Soul by digital artist, Bruce Rolf.

Finally I would like to acknowledge the generosity of fellow spiritual counselors who freely shared their knowledge and enabled me to develop a 21st century version of counseling that can be done over the internet using telepathy. I am grateful to Dexter Gelfand, Roger Boswarva, Hank Levin, Maxim Lebedev, and Mikhail Federov for sharing their discoveries and encouraging me to share mine.

Last, but not least, I want to thank Dr Sam Saadat, and Dr. Sudhendu Choubey for their excellent work in keeping my well-worn body alive and functioning so I could finish this book.

They and the staff members at the Tri-Area Clinic in Floyd and Carilion Hospitals in Roanoke and Radford are fine examples of caring medical care in action.

This book would not have happened without all of your help.

APPENDIX

SPIRITUAL RESCUE TECHNOLOGY

Spiritual Rescue Technology was developed through years of research into spiritual behavior. It is basically the collected notes of 10 years of research and was developed for my world wide spiritual counseling practice.

It represented a complete departure from traditional spiritual counseling as practiced by the Church of Scientology, Ron's Org, and other Scientology offshoots.

This accumulation of information includes thousands of forum entries and two earlier books, Introducing Spiritual Rescue Technology and Using Spiritual Technology.

Spiritual Rescue Technology is different from many other spiritual practices in that we recognize that spiritual beings are alive, they are intelligent, many of them used to have bodies but don't now, and they have goals and purposes that may or may not be aligned with our own.

You are a spirit and you will be working with other spirits and aligning them toward a goal that you choose. As you might imagine, this can be a challenge, but we have already done the research to make it possible.

The secret of Spiritual Rescue Technology's success and ease of use is in understanding that caring communication is essential in rescuing spiritual beings from the problems they can be stuck in.

This is the whole secret of this technology:

You communicate In a caring way with spiritual beings, get them to let go of incidents that are affecting them adversely, and set them free to create new futures.

The beings who choose to help you will give you greatly expanded abilities if you organize them into a well-drilled team and recognize their abilities and use them.

They can give you access to new abilities in fields like: Art, music, engineering, warfare, literature, philosophy, politics, and science.

Links to books on Spiritual Rescue Technology:
Introducing Spiritual Rescue Technology:
https://www.amazon.com/Introducing-Spiritual-Rescue-Technology-Practical-ebook/dp/B00NJTIJZW

Using Spiritual Technology:
https://www.amazon.com/Using-Spiritual-Rescue-Technology-Connections-ebook/dp/B00WVQ2DL0

Links to Websites on Spiritual Rescue Technology:
https://www.facebook.com/groups/spiritualrescuetechnology/
https://caring-communication.com/SRTHOME/
https://www.facebook.com/SRTCounseling/
https://caring-communication.com/forum/

Links To Videos on Spiritual Rescue Technology:
https://vimeo.com/210061081
https://vimeo.com/213361463

SUCCESSES FROM USING SPIRITUAL RESCUE TECHNOLOGY ON SELF OR ON OTHERS

The Technology Works
A couple of days ago I read your site and started working with my spirits.

I'm amazed at the results of the first sessions: moving away from my body and aware of myself as independent of my body and able to "see", "hear", etc. as a spirit and not as a body; uncontrolled laughter as a result of getting rid of so much long-term upset; the rapid disappearance of aches, pains and other unwanted body sensations, etc.

This can have quite some effect on my life, and I'll let you know how it goes or when I may need your help.

Body Problem
I have had a lower back problem for 60 years, ever since I jumped off an armored vehicle in cold weather. It usually runs for a week or two, and I hobble around until it subsides.

When I was receiving spiritual counseling in a church, I realized it could be psychosomatic, and that caused it to disappear completely for many years. Recently it has returned and I finally realized it was not mine!

Getting in communication with spirits in the area has enabled me to relieve the pain within minutes. There seems to be many spirits in this area that go into action and turn on my pain in cold weather (something about being injured in a really cold environment), but I now feel confident that I can keep this under control and will eventually handle all of the spirits involved.

Moving into My Own Identity

I hardly know where to begin on describing what has occurred in my latest sessions! I will attempt to put it into human words.

The feeling that I have always had that I could not have success in life is lifting. I am truly moving into my own identity. My admiration for life is at an all-time high. I have this feeling of expansiveness that I have not felt in a long, long time. I am once again becoming indestructible and invincible. I can more and more be the person who I really am. This is so spiritual that I do not have a datum of comparable magnitude to compare it with.

I had a very interesting realization that we are really composite beings. You are you, plus your spirits. You are the master of your harem. You can be the effect of your spirits, or you can be cause and grant them the respect that they deserve as real beings and acknowledge them. I like the cause viewpoint. It is much more fun—not only for you, but for them.

You have no idea how much affinity was flowed back to me from my spirits from my last session. It was like a gush of water from a river. My space got cleaned up, and my spirits were so happy to be in such a clean space. Also the relief that they experienced from the incident was just absolutely overwhelming to me. It actually brought tears of joy. That is what they flowed at me simple joy and relief!

Shift in Viewpoint
Just thought I should mention a win that I had today after session:
I feel as though I have actually joined the human race. I am not sure what that all means, but I felt as though I have been somewhat disconnected from humanity for some time now—like I just did not quite fit in. I'm not sure when it began, but it was a long time ago. I now feel as though I am actually part of the human race. I can have so much more affinity for the rest of us, and I am sure that will increase as time goes by.

I am not quite sure how to communicate fully how, because of today's session, I feel as though I have allowed myself to be part of this group known as mankind. I was holding myself back, not wanting to "infect" others. I can now experience all the joy and pain of being human.

WOW! Sometimes these Earth words do not do justice to the wins and realizations that you can have in session.

Becoming Oneself
So here are my latest wins. Things that used to be on automatic, I am now aware of actually doing. I am becoming cause over my life and existence. I am actually aware of being aware. May not sound like much to you, but seems big to me.
Then, I am getting more and more in control of my emotions and thoughts—like I can really just be ME.

Mitigating a Serious Physical Condition
I have had back surgery and have more problems than I should: several ruptured discs, compression fracture, broken hip that took 18 months to almost heal. Around the house, I use a cane. Out and about, I use a fancy walker with big tires, brakes, basket, and a seat—just like old people use. LOL!

I am old. I was certain this would be my life from now on. I had done other spiritual counseling and had gotten better to a degree that amazed me; only I still hurt most of the time.

David had me take a look and found a cluster of spirits in my spine. I had not found it before and did not even suspect it. David saw it and got me to spot it and handle it. It is gone and I have not used my walker or cane for a week now. I suspect it will continue.

The pain in my spine is less than it has been in 30 years. Oh, I am not going to run a marathon, yet!

I have admired and liked David for 33 years. Now I think he is magic. He knows the technology and how to apply it to the beings he is helping. That is a good thing, Martha. Peace Love & Harmony. RB

Overcoming Fears of Not Getting Out in Time
I'm new to Spiritual Rescue Technology. I discovered it last week and did a few solo sessions. Then I had an intro session from David St. Lawrence which knocked my socks off, and I got a really good idea how to do this and how uncomplicated and how fast this can be. It's conceptual. Thoughts are instantaneous.

Yesterday we woke up to find that we had wildfires raging away on three sides of us but far enough away so we weren't in immediate danger. I started to get "nervous" but realized that this was not my feeling so I got it under control. Or thought I did. A motorcycle policeman came and told us to evacuate. That was when I kind of lost it—or someone did.

I knew we HAD to leave RIGHT NOW or it would be too late. I just KNEW it would be too late. My daughter was packing all this pointless stuff, and I kept thinking, "She's like the Jews who didn't get out of Germany in time because they felt they had time to pack and that nothing bad was going to happen." I put my stuff and my dog in my car and I went and sat in a Home Depot until we got the all clear.

I have this "thing" about Nazi concentration camps and what was done to the Jews during WWII. I know I wasn't there at that time because I am able to remember my past lifetime, and I know I was safely living in southeastern Pennsylvania at that time. However, I have thoughts about Nazi concentration camps ALL THE TIME.

It finally hit me! I have a group of spirits who have been with me since 1945 when they died in a Nazi concentration camp! I acknowledged them and their relief was incredible. We ran Spiritual Rescue Technology on the incident, and they said what happened was they didn't listen to the warnings. Instead they listened to their beloved Rabbi who told them, "God will take care of us. He won't let anything happen to us."

Anyway, my new/old friends are now enjoying themselves in northern California somewhere in a redwood forest. They're up there where it's very peaceful, mingling with all the tourists, and I don't feel this irrational urgency about "getting out before it's too late."

Handling Spirits Connected to a Person Who is Not Present
Spiritual Rescue Technology is amazing. I had a session with David last week, and he helped me to crack a "trauma" of long duration in this lifetime of mine.

Sure enough, an spirit was involved and traumatized my relationship with my mother and my older brother.

Soon after the session, I talked to my mother (I called her) to see how she's doing, and it was the calmest conversation for years. And yesterday my older brother contacted me and asked for some help (he very seldom calls and even less asks for help or a favor).

When you love someone but it is somehow impossible for you to project this love or establish positive communication lines and understanding, it may have to do with some spirits at play.

It is really interesting to find out, time and time again, that the spirits are trying, in their own way of thinking, to help.

Handling Chatter In My Head
Did you ever wonder where your "thoughts" originate from? If you had this chatter in your head like me before then you should really know what is the origin of this chatter.

I knew it a little bit longer, that chatter or thoughts can't be mine, but wasn't able to silence them! While doing SRT in solo session and with David, the chatter almost disappeared and I am sure that it is soon completely gone.

The surprise of this was, that I now have some handicraft skills I didn't have before! If you are clear in your head you are able to do tasks you were not able to do before.

I can't explain this, but I was a loser at handicraft skills.

After our last session I haven't found this win before. It came a little bit later on the surface, so I had to write.

Out of thin air I was able to rebuild a cupboard without any manual or do drillings for a clothes tree in a floor for one of my relatives.

But most of all, it is important that people know that their chatter can cease by doing solo sessions in SRT-style or doing a session with you. This chatter would otherwise cause some real trouble to people who are not able to cope such appearances anymore. With SRT and it is feasible to let it go and that is a great relief for everybody.

That was my contribution to this awesome method. LW

****

You will find more information about the development of Spiritual Rescue Technology and examples of SRT sessions on the SRT website:
https://caring-communication.com/SRTHOME/

When you start using SRT on yourself and others, you may wish to read the stories being shared on a forum established for students and users of Spiritual Rescue Technology.

Registration is required to read the private sections of the forum:
https://caring-communication.com/forum/

Alphabetical Index

249

T

ABOUT THE AUTHOR

David St Lawrence lives in the Blue Ridge Mountains of Southwest Virginia with his wife Gretchen and their collection of cats.

After 43 years of designing and working with computers and trying to make sense of corporate life, he decided to research the underlying causes for the insanity of modern corporate life and discovered how spiritual beings influence our lives.

The first discovery was that most people were literally haunted by unhappy spirits who affected their judgment and their sanity by giving them distracting messages.

He developed a conversational method of helping the unhappy spirits to go free and start new lives. This allowed his clients to experience a new freedom for the first time in their lives and allowed them to expand their careers and achieve their goals.

He was then able to show clients how to manage their spiritual companions and make them into helpful teams so that achieving goals became almost effortless.

This book, Talking To Spirits, is intended to be the first step in enabling you to teach yourselves about spirits, and enrich your lives by harnessing the power of your spiritual companions to help you achieve the goals you choose.

Made in the USA
Las Vegas, NV
09 April 2022

47144931R00148